Near-Death Exp
Are Real

MW01484642

But Only for Survivors!

William Pillow

Also by William Pillow:

Love and Immortality: Long Journey of My Heart
Meet Yourself Again for the First Time
Mind, Body, & Spirit: Challenges of Science and Faith
Souls Are Real: Death Is Not

Acknowledgments

Our Creator, my birth family, and our married family naturally come first for my gratitude in being able to write this book. I especially express my love, respect, and appreciation for my beloved wife, Betty, whose soul has passed into Heaven. I give special thanks to our son, Brad, and to our daughter, Val, for their loving personal support and encouragement for my writing, and for their tolerance of whatever my spiritual research revealed.

I am indebted, as are we all, to the survivors of sudden cardiac arrest who reported on their near-death experiences. Without their fearless testimonies and the progress of dedicated researchers, the rest of us would still fear death and be wondering about that place that religions call "Heaven."

I am particularly grateful to those researchers and academicians who were willing to risk their personal standing among peers and colleagues by breaking through the glass walls that enclose and restrain science and scientists from contemplating and exploring what is sometimes called the world beyond the "material" reality.

I owe a debt of gratitude to psychotherapist Michael Newton for his extensive research and books that helped me move from being a devoted skeptic about the paranormal for most of my life. It is only through his dedication—and the kind permission from his publisher, Llewellyn World, to reproduce some of his findings here, that this book was made possible.

I also appreciate the work that psychiatrist Brian Weiss has done in hypnotically regressing thousands of patients to their souls' past lives (i.e., past reincarnations). Only there did they find and heal traumatic soul memories which were otherwise inaccessible consciously in this life. His office kindly gave permissions for quotations from his books.

I am indebted, as are we all, to the pioneers in prenatal and perinatal psychology and in biobehavioral sciences for their dedicated pursuit of better understanding of the biological roots of human behavior. I hope that, in time, these advances will be more widely accepted in all parts of our society, so that our young people can benefit throughout their early lives.

Special recognition and gratitude is given for the following permissions from the publisher of Michael Newton's books, whose pioneering efforts were instrumental in encouraging my quest for meaning and in helping build credibility for our souls:

Journey of Souls by Michael Newton, Ph.D. © 1994 Llewellyn Worldwide, Ltd. 2143 Wooddale Drive, Woodbury, MN 55125-2989. Used by permission of the publisher. All rights reserved.

Destiny of Souls by Michael Newton, Ph.D. © 2000 Llewellyn Worldwide, Ltd. 2143 Wooddale Drive, Woodbury, MN 55125-2989. Used by permission of the publisher. All rights reserved.

Life Between Lives: Hypnotherapy for Spiritual Regression by Michael Newton, Ph.D. © 2004 Llewellyn Worldwide, Ltd. 2143 Wooddale Drive, Woodbury, MN 55125-2989. Used by permission of the publisher. All rights reserved.

Memories of the Afterlife: Life Between Lives Stories of Personal Transformation by Michael Newton, Ph.D. © 2009 Llewellyn Worldwide, Ltd. 2143 Wooddale Drive, Woodbury, MN55125-2989. Used by permission of the publisher. All rights reserved.

Introduction

Contents

Bibliography

Introduction

In case you still are wondering about this book's title, "Near-Death Experiences *Are* Real: But Only for Survivors!" it has two meanings. The obvious one is that non-survivors die. But the implicit meaning is that—despite this book and any conceivable human research—near-death experiences (NDEs) will *never* become perceptible to normal human beings!

Therefore this book is radically different from any other book you have ever *seen, read, or heard about.* It dares to challenge everyone's beliefs about the so-called "reality." Although the book reads like science fiction, everything you read here is as *factual* as is humanly possible.

For example, you cannot *personally* perceive the electromagnetic waves that invisibly surround us to carry Internet information and communications! So this book will introduce you to *another* kind of *humanly* imperceptible energy that facilitates near-death experiences—just as *real* as your Internet! Once you accept that, and why and how they occur, you might welcome them as much as you did the Internet.

Reality today—that which is defined by our five physical senses (i.e., see, touch, hear, smell, and taste) —might seem restrictive at times. But only if you realize that science, medicine, and religion are being confronted by increasing enigmas. So this book seeks plausible answers for near-death experiences that dare to go beyond the boundaries of research that have been established.

Yet, you still must be the judge of what you read here. For example, because the cause of NDEs (i.e., sudden cardiac arrest) kills *more* people than survive, this book also details theories of mortal death that offer hope for the so-called "afterlife."

So some of you *actually* might look forward to what you learn here, because one of those "plausible answers" addresses whether mortal death is *final* for human beings. Another answer explains why "near-death" experiences (NDE's) are *real* for NDE *survivors.* Yet another answer suggests that recent revelations from our soul's hypnotically regressed "life-between-lives" (i.e., Heaven) offers a *dramatically* more personal perspective about God—than has ever been possible in the past.

These details also show why the Eternal Almighty is the One and Only Supreme Power—regardless of what names we humans use for It—such as God, Allah, Yahweh, or any other term of esteem and respect. If the term "It" shocks you, this acknowledges that The Creator now seems quite different from the perspective created by sacred scriptures two millennia ago. Spirit entities have no innate gender since they do *not* reproduce as humans do. Furthermore, they are *not* material beings like us.

However, it is very likely that readers who have survived a near-death experience, *or* have had a hypnotic regression to their soul's past-life memories, will be more familiar with this book's content than those who have *not.* This seems true because those who *have* will be able to *accept* the reality of our God-given souls *and* the dependence of near-death experiences upon our souls.

This book therefore reveals nothing threatening. Instead, it offers an understanding how that which seems enigmatic might really prove beneficial for human lives on Earth.

Chapter One

Preliminary Thoughts

Human religions around the world are confronting various contemporary challenges to their longstanding emphasis on faith. Yet, this has taken less than half a century, as compared to the many centuries over which multiple human religions developed. Yet, the term "human" reflects how, over that long period, the significance of a Supreme Power seems to have dwindled substantially from what humanity had forever held in awe.

Down through time, our ancestors seem to have sensed hidden truths as they buried their loved ones. They sustained a hope that has forever dwelt in the mind of man. At its heart, our forefathers instinctively believed in a Supreme Power. But you may be surprised how long ago mankind acknowledged that unseen forces exist—and they even symbolized their beliefs and fears through some sort of structure and worship.

Religion

Until the last ice age loosed its grip about 9,600 BC, our ancestors were largely hunters and gatherers who still lived in hut settlements of a few hundred people. But something happened around that time which *National Geographic* magazine's cover story called "The Birth of Religion," in an article by Charles Mann. That cover also claimed "The World's First Temple." However, the term "religion" would not be needed for *another* ten thousand years.

In the context of time, the Great Pyramid of Giza and Stonehenge had not been built for *seven* thousand years. Confucius, Buddha, Socrates, Aristotle, Jesus, and Mohammed would not have been born until about two millennia later. This ancient "temple's" discovery therefore dated back over eleven thousand years.

The invention of writing about five thousand years ago (i.e., 3200 BC) in the Near East helped chronicle the history of "religion." The Pyramid Texts from ancient Egypt are one of the oldest known "religious" inscriptions, dating around four thousand years ago (i.e., 2300 BC). The Dead Sea Scrolls originated around two thousand years later (i.e., 250 BC).

Faith in the Divine

Perhaps the obvious *lack* of *humanly perceptible* evidence of a Supreme Power made it more difficult to justify faith among the masses in modern society. So much so that *Time* magazine's April 8, 1966 cover asked, "Is God Dead?"

Nevertheless, many people *privately* do admit disappointment in the results of their personal prayers. *Publicly*, many people criticize a *purportedly* loving God for failures to prevent widespread death, destruction, and upheaval from natural calamities.

God Does Not Create Miracles—You Do! is a fascinating approach to the achievement of human potential. Its author, Yahuda Berg, is Co-Director of the Kabbalah Center in Los Angeles. The Kabbalah is a Hebrew source of wisdom that stretches back to ancient Babylon. Berg's book offers an encouraging perspective about attitudes toward, and applications of, human potential.

He writes, "According to Kabbalah, God is an infinitely powerful and positive force. *You* create your own miracles when *you successfully connect* to this infinite force of goodness—

connection being the key concept here ... it is your effort, your work, your physical, emotional, and spiritual exertion that brings about the miracles in your physical world.

A Roman Emperor's Influence

But the 1980s revived two *humanly* perceptible attributes of God. Yet, these remain unknown to many people, because they were struck from Christian theology in 553 CE. Nevertheless, two psychoanalysts *accidentally* discovered that God provides these to every human that ever lives on Earth!

Long ago, the Father of the Early Church, Origen of Alexandria (185-254 CE) was the first person since the Apostle Paul to develop a system of theology around the teachings of Jesus. Yet, Origen was also an ardent defender of *souls* and *reincarnation.* But in 553 CE at the Second Council of Constantinople, the Eastern Roman Emperor Justinian cleverly removed them from Christian doctrine. He also excommunicated Origen from the Roman Catholic Church. The concepts of God-given souls and reincarnation therefore languished until the 1980s.

You may wonder about Justinian's reason for removing souls and reincarnation from Christian theology. In his book *Reincarnation in Christianity: A New Vision of the Role of Rebirth in Christian Thought,* Geddes MacGregor delves into the annals of Christian history to demonstrate that Christian doctrine and reincarnation are not mutually exclusive belief systems. MacGregor believes that the Church rejected reincarnation not for theological reasons but as a threat to the Church and to Rome at a time when their institutional strength was crucial. He is Emeritus Distinguished Professor of Philosophy at the University of Southern California.

Serendipity

Yet, as a result of two psychoanalysts' *shocking* discovery for accessing memories of our soul's past lives (i.e., incarnations), you now can learn more about the *reality* of not only souls and reincarnation, but also God and Heaven. Souls, like God and Heaven, obviously are part of a reality that is indiscernible to humans. That "reality" seems to stretch far beyond the current paradigm of scientific materialism. The "spiritual forces" of that expanded reality may even be cosmic and eternal. Naturally, you probably find this hard to accept ... or even imagine!

So remember this claim from the Introduction: "So this book will introduce you to another kind of humanly imperceptible *energy* that facilitates spiritual phenomena that are just as *real* as your Internet—to near-death experience (NDE) survivors!"

Experiential Evidence

The Centers for Disease Control and Prevention (CDC) defines "experiential evidence as "This type of evidence is based on the professional insight, understanding, skill, and expertise that is accumulated over time and is often referred to as intuitive or tacit knowledge." This is published in the CDC *Guide to Understanding Evidence,* which also says "The Best Available Research Evidence is widely accepted as the most commonly used type of evidence in fields ranging from medicine to psychology."

The experiential evidence detailed later is this book in this book—that our souls incarnate in the womb and move from our expiring physical body back into the eternal realm of the afterlife—seems hard to dispute. With this realization, it is increasingly difficult for anyone to deny that both souls and Heaven are part of the expanded reality of the Divine. However, this may be beyond the reach of human science to prove *or* disprove. It would then remain an everlasting mystery of life.

Brief History of Souls and Reincarnation

The idea that you have a soul may surprise you, especially if you seldom, if ever, heard the term "soul" mentioned. Even if you are a "religious" person, you certainly never heard it explained. Undoubtedly, you never understood that it has such an intrinsic role in your earthly life. But consider from the discussion on soul consciousness that our souls were created by the Divine Source to exemplify God's wisdom, power, and unconditional love.

Early Greek philosophers theorized and debated the nature of the soul. One of the most incisive analyses of this is John Bussanich's 2013 "Rebirth and Eschatology in Plato and Plotinus" in the book *Philosophy and Salvation in Greek Religion*. There you would find concepts that sound familiar after you complete our book. An example is Plato's "River of Lethe" (i.e., Veil of Forgetfulness).

Also, in Bussanich's words, "The implicit constructive message of Platonic myth [i.e., writing] is that the rebirth cycle will continue without end until one becomes detached from the desires and needs of the lower parts of the soul and seeks wisdom and virtue, even in the most constrained circumstances." Bussanich adds a statement of legitimacy for Plato's views, "I cannot defend the claim here, but the abundant evidence of mystical experiences in the [Platonic] dialogues demonstrates that Plato was intimately familiar with the transcendent worlds."

Persistent Enigma

Meanwhile, as you will read in the next chapter, so-called "near-death" (NDE) experiences apparently have happened since ancient history. But, as you will also find, dedicated research across the world has been *unable* to explain what NDE survivors claim happened to them. Even they had doubts at first—until their number grew to millions around the world. Now everyone wants to know "Are NDEs real?"

So it may be important that you try to develop a more holistic approach for the possible meaning *behind* the many ideas in this book—connect the dots, so to speak. This book promises a plausible answer to the question, "Are near-death experiences real?" Yet, that answer is multifaceted rather than simple.

"Hidden" NDE's

Millions of NDE survivors realize the obvious—that near-death experiences are *not* perceptible to any other living human being. Furthermore, researchers are *unable* to simulate the *core* near-death experience. What is it, therefore, about the NDE experience? Hint: Is he or she *still* alive during the NDE experience—as he or she later claims?

Contemporary Dilemmas

Over time, however, the Hebrew Old Testament Book of Genesis became the subject of debate between literalists and scientists. Perhaps fostered by several millennia of differences in their contexts, disagreements occurred on several points. Two of the most prominent seem to be creation and evolution.

Creation

Advances in astronomy and cosmology seemingly allowed researchers to claim the creation of the universe, as we know it, about fourteen *billion* years ago. This apparently is considered a "natural" event, unrelated to a Supreme Power.

Remarkably, the statistics of the universe are almost incredible. Although it is estimated that two trillion galaxies exist in the universe, each with a billion stars, these represent only five percent of the visible universe. Researchers think most of the cosmos is made up of matter and energy that cannot be "sensed" with conventional instruments, leading to the names "dark matter" and "dark energy."

As inconceivable as that is, the Big Bang concept apparently erupted from a "singularity." Theoretically, "black holes" have a gravitational field so intense that no matter or radiation can escape it. Dying stars, for example, would be sucked in. The product, so to speak, is a type of singularity.

Yet, new theories continue to abound about the Big Bang. To discuss them here seems worthless as an aspect of this book. Yet three haunting questions remain. The eruption of a singularity was *not* the prime "beginning," was it? Its massive contents must have existed previously in some other way. Also, science may deny a spiritual Creation, but what proof is there that God did *not* use such power and energy in creating everything that is? Since researchers have not yet found a final border to the universe, might it be infinite?

Life Essentials

A young University of Illinois graduate student named Stanley Miller published the results of an experiment in which he showed that amino acids could be produced in a spark chamber. Since amino acids are the precursors to proteins, this led scientists to believe that the creation of life itself was within their grasp. Although scientists continue trying to produce life in a test tube, no one has succeeded.

DNA has been an essential part of life forms from the dawn of creation. The DNA evidence suggests that these basic mechanisms controlling biological form and protein production became established before or during the evolution of multicellular organisms and have been conserved with little modification ever since. Adding to science's dilemma for producing test tube life therefore was the question of how these first genes developed.

It seems conceivable that the information provided in DNA was part of the creation of life forms. Werner Gitt's seminal book *In the Beginning was Information: A Scientist Explains the Incredible Design in Nature* stresses that there is "a unique coding system ... of biological information ... in each genome." Further, Gitt quotes the conclusion of the seventh International Conference on the Origins of Life held in Mainz, Germany: "There is no known law of nature, no known process, and no known sequence of events which can cause information to originate by itself in nature."

Several characteristics about this biological information illustrate Gitt's claim "The coding system used for living beings is optimal from an engineering standpoint." First, it can be described as three different forms: "constructional/creative, operational, and communication."

Also, the information can be distinguished as "copied, reproduced, or creative." Qualitatively, the information ranges from "extremely important" to "trivial" or "harmful." Quantitatively, it varies according to "semantic quality, relevance, timeliness, accessibility, existence, and comprehensibility. This strengthens the argument that it was a case of purposeful design rather that a [lucky] chance."

In case DNA's small size might appear insignificant as a major barrier to the creation of life by scientists, some details about DNA may help us realize the enormity of intelligence incorporated in DNA. Scientists found that DNA contains an exquisite "language" composed of some three billion genetic letters. Lee Strobel's book *The Case for a Creator* contains a statement by Stephen Meyer, director of the Center for Science and Culture at the Discovery Institute in Seattle, WA "One of the most extraordinary discoveries of the twentieth century was that DNA actually stores information—the detailed instructions for assembling proteins—in the form of a four-character digital code." Meyer elaborated on this in his book *Signature in the Cell: DNA and the Evidence for Intelligent Design.*

It is hard to fathom, but the amount of information in human DNA is roughly equivalent to twelve sets of the *Encyclopedia Britannica*—an incredible three hundred and eighty-four volumes' worth of detailed information that would fill forty-eight feet of library shelves! Molecular biologist Michael Denton's book *Evolution: A Theory in Crisis* said "In their actual size—which is only two millionths of a millimeter thick—a teaspoon of DNA could contain all the information needed to build the proteins for all the species of organisms that have ever lived on the earth, and there would still be enough room left for all the information in every book ever written."

Even if science ever solves the dilemma of how DNA originated in life forms on earth, there remains the inevitable and inexplicable question: where did all this information come from?

In Michael Newton's most recent book *Memories of the Afterlife: Life Between Lives Stories of Personal Transformation* he wrote, "I believe the forces of intelligent creation go far beyond the religious concept of an anthropomorphic god (i.e., having a human form or human attributes.) These spiritual forces ... indicate that creation of intelligent energy is so vast in our universe as to be incomprehensible to the human mind."

Evolution

In 1859, English naturalist Charles Darwin reported changes he observed physical or behavioral changes in animals of the same species, which he attributed to so-called natural selection." The Church of England's scientific establishment reacted against the book, while liberal Anglicans strongly supported Darwin's natural selection as an instrument of God's design. Yet, this disagreement persisted until now.

Obviously, genetic understanding came more than a century later. Now, it is known that aspects of gene control of future generations also can happen without a change in the underlying DNA sequence. This occurs through a process known as "epigenetics." It involves the ways genes work, so to speak. Influences can modify a parent's genes and that modification is passed on to offspring.

But this might have become possible, in the context of this book, as part of God's Grand Plan for humanity. After creating everything that is, the Eternal Almighty may have seen fit to allow species of life on Earth to modify their and their offspring's ability to survive and procreate on Earth by adapting to their changing environments.

Birth Mothers

Some readers may feel that this section is out of character for this book—and others may object to the apparent stereotyping of parenting responsibility. Yet, you just learned that epigenetics can significantly an offspring's future. In a later chapter, you will read the significance of our right cerebral hemisphere, including the words of the eminent clinical neuropsychologist Allan Schore. He writes, "It is the right hemisphere and its implicit [i.e., unconscious] functions … that are truly dominant in human existence. Over the lifespan, the early-forming unconscious implicit self [i.e., right hemisphere] continues to develop to more complexity, and it operates in qualitatively different ways from the later-forming conscious explicit self [i.e., left hemisphere]."

He is an ardent advocate for the very young child's bond with his or her birth mother, also called "attachment" in professional literature. In that later chapter, you will also find that the young child's right hemisphere is functional for his or her first two to three years of life, while the left hemisphere does not become functional until after that period. This increases the significance of those early years for the child's future lifetime.

Reactive attachment disorder (RAD) is one of the few officially recognized psychiatric disorders that can be applied to infants. It follows children into adulthood when it was not appropriately treated in childhood. Adult RAD has been characterized as having trouble being genuine in friendships and romantic relationships. This results from having difficulty showing empathy, remorse, trust, and compassion—four traits whose deprivation might be troubling in social, business, and professional life, especially from inability or difficulties in forming secure relationships. It has been postulated that as many as one-half of all Americans are diagnosable with Adult Attachment Disorder (AAD).

Since the birth mother has been the fetus' physical, emotional, nutritional, and security support for about nine months, the newborn and infant logically have developed a set of expectations from its birth mother. Obviously, family or environmental disruptions from change, unexpected or otherwise, can foster RAD, as can shifting from the birth mother to a different significant other as primary caregiver.

Providential?

This term, "providential" (i.e., involving divine intervention), may provoke an "ah-ha" moment, suspecting that the book *is* religious. But do you consider God a "human" religion? Moreover, if God were involved, could understanding about the near-death experience ever happen, with science's current material paradigm for reality?

Maybe a word of two about the author will convince you otherwise. My family and I—until my beloved wife, Betty, passed over in 2009—were Sunday school and church members everywhere we have ever lived. But her increasingly serious illnesses began to confront me with new uncertainties about our separation through death. As a scientist (i.e., pharmacist), I realized that doctors knew little for sure about death. They would not discuss it, but call it a "treatment failure." Even less seemed certain about religions. Also, unfortunately, many religions seem to relate the afterlife to God's misperceived expectations while we are alive.

But my personal conviction about the Supreme Power is that Its love is *unconditional!* My use of the term "Its" reflects that God, souls, and any other spirits are genderless— except that souls in Heaven are said to often adopt the lifelike appearance of their favorite past-life host.

So I started a spiritual quest, which I continue even today. Incidentally, I found that I learned only to the extent that I questioned beliefs I had been taught in my earlier life—I now am 86. But I've never had an NDE or been hypnotically regressed.

The Future?

Hopefully, as you read this book, you will be able to consider the value of our God-given souls to us and to our families—in our lives on Earth and when our physical bodies die.

With religious institutions facing challenges of contemporary changes in society, those institutions have an opportunity to emphasize the spiritual bedrock for the individual and his or her family that their souls can play in their lives and "death."

Maybe, as or after you read this book, you may agree that this new awareness of our immortal souls also offers a more credible perspective about God.

So the next chapter introduces you to near-death experiences.

Chapter Two

The Reality of Near-Death Experiences

As long as humankind has existed on Earth, human beings likely have died from sudden cardiac arrests that are today acknowledged as near-death experiences (NDEs). The Classical Greek philosopher, Plato (427-348 BCE), wrote about an apparent "near-death" experience in his treatise *Republic*, a soldier thought dead on the battlefield but was later revived:

> "He [i.e., the soldier] describes a journey from darkness to light, accompanied by guides, a moment of judgment, feelings of peace and joy, and visions of extraordinary beauty and happiness."

NDE Survivor Claims

For years, even survivors of near-death experiences doubted what most of them experienced, so eerie did it seem. In a later chapter, you will read about Baptist minister Don Piper, who refused to tell anyone about his "visit to Heaven" for two years. But in recent times, however, more survivors have told their physicians.

So, as consistent NDE reports were increasingly heard, more physicians agreed that survivors' incredible claims *could* have a clinical impact. Yet, skeptics and advocates continued to debate the cause *and* nature of "near-death experiences."

Unless you have had—or know someone who has had—a near-death experience, this book may sound like science fiction! But millions of people around the world have *actually* had NDEs and lived to tell about it. But, as you will read later, more people *have* died from its cause than lived, because emergency help was not quick enough, appropriate, or sufficient.

But perhaps the weirdest feeling that survivors consistently describe is that "he" or "she" had *totally* separated from "his" or "her" lifeless body. In other words, "he" or "she" *still* felt alive—and could hear, see, think, and *remember*. But their accurate details were astounding—about what was happening with the lifeless body nearby, the medical team, and even readings on clinical status monitors!

In other words, the "real me" separated from my body. Of course, you might doubt that it is the "real you", since you consciously have worked long and hard to achieve the life, position, and standing that you have.

Yet, this book *not only* describes but also *illustrates*—from *inside* an NDE experience itself—what *actually* happened. The book also explains why *only* the NDE survivor is aware what happened to "him" or "her"—*no* bystander, relative, or even a medical professional can *humanly* perceive the separated "him" or "her."

This *fact* is based upon a different kind of reality discussed in the next section. It is called "incorporeal" or "incorporeality." It is a *real* state of existence that is defined as "having no material form, body, or substance." Yet, this kind of existence has a historical and spiritual basis, as you will read later.

Exploring Realities

In order for the reader to fully contemplate the true nature of near-death experiences, he or she must consider that so-called "reality" might reach *beyond* what our five physical senses can detect: see, feel, taste, hear, or smell. The Introduction included an example that you cannot *personally* perceive—the electromagnetic waves that enable your Internet communications! But, as the Introduction also said, everything you read here is as factual as is humanly possible. So everything in this book should be reassuring of life on Earth and that death is not the finality we usually fear.

You therefore are asked to consider two real states of existence upon which this book is based. Both are beyond the bounds of academic science—and may remain there. One, discussed here, is called "incorporeal" (i.e., having no material form or substance). Said another way, God creates each soul as a "bundle" of spiritual energy, imbued with providential capabilities, all of which is incorporeal. The other real state of existence will be discussed in a later chapter.

Background for Incorporeality

Historically, pagan gods of the ancient world often were personifications of nature or forces for good or evil. So the idea of "incorporeal" (i.e., lacking material form or substance) was used to distinguish God in Judaism, Christianity, and Islam. Elizabeth Grosz's new book *The Incorporeal: Ontology, Ethics, and the Limits of Materialism* seems very applicable here.

That book's Amazon review includes, "From its origins in the writings of the Stoics, the first thoroughgoing materialists, another view has acknowledged that no forms of materialism can be completely self-inclusive ... [and] the world preexists the evolution of the human, and its material and incorporeal forces are the conditions for all forms of life, human and nonhuman alike."

Moreover, as Robert Renehan, Professor of Classics at UCLA Santa Barbara, concludes in his definitive paper, "On the Greek Origins of the Concepts of Incorporeality and Immateriality," "For almost two thousand years, the concepts of incorporeality and immateriality were central in much Western philosophical and theological speculation on such problems as the nature of God, Soul, [and] Intellect. When all is said and done, it must be recognized that one man was responsible for the creation of an ontology that culminates in incorporeal Being as the truest and highest reality. That man was Plato."

Incorporeal existence therefore applies to our God-given souls as well as to near-death experiences. The key to understanding anything incorporeal (i.e., non-material) is that it is invisible to human perception and is *not* detectable by any device yet created by humankind.

NDE Survivor Claims

Readers who are *not* aware of what some NDE survivors describe may doubt or even disavow such claims. But please understand that *not* every person who is resuscitated from a cardiac arrest had a near-death experience.

NDEs consist of two different kinds of personal experiences, usually one *or* the other. One involves feeling separated from a lifeless body—yet still *alive*—and moving some distance, typically above the resuscitation effort. The other involves moving through a tube or tunnel and "visiting Heaven." This experience usually includes being met by a brilliant light of love as well as reunion with previously departed loved ones. "He" or "she" may be told, "You have to go back. Your time is not yet."

To some extent, the difference between the two kinds seems to depend upon how long the physical body remains comatose. Of course, *any* such kind of *sensory* experience might seem doubtful, especially what has been claimed.

One claim seems more common, however, wherein the survivor feels that his or her "self" separated from his or her body and simply rose up to a corner of the ceiling. Yet, if and when the victim's body is resuscitated, NDE survivors feel "sucked back" into their body. Perhaps remarkable, too, is the overall transformation of attitudes about life on Earth that survivors who "visit Heaven" bring back with them. This will be discussed in a later chapter.

Failure to Survive a Sudden Cardiac Arrest

Yet, when discussing "near-death" experiences, perhaps we simply do not *realize* the overwhelming number of sudden cardiac arrest victims who do *not* survive! According to the Sudden Cardiac Arrest Foundation (SCAF), the number of deaths *each year* from sudden cardiac arrest is shocking. It roughly amounts to the number who die from Alzheimer's disease, assault with firearms, breast cancer, cervical cancer, colorectal cancer, diabetes, HIV, house fires, prostate cancer, suicides, and motor vehicle accidents *combined!*

So, as you will read more about this later, *sudden* cardiac arrest *is* a first step in dying— lack of oxygen causes the brain to initiate the process of dying. That is why near-death experiences are so amazing. How could it be? Survivors claim that the *real* "me" separated from the body, but nobody witnessed it but "him" or "her"? Moreover, NDE survivors remembered what happened while their body was apparently dead!

There are two classic examples. In one, an emergency nurse took out the victim's dentures and put them in the top drawer of a utility cabinet. When he asked for them after recovering, no one could find them. When they told him, he said, "A nurse put them in the top drawer of that cabinet!" The other example involved a beautiful gold pen. The victim's cardiologist wore it in the pocket of his medical jacket. But it slipped out without his knowledge, as he bent over the victim, and it rolled under a medical cabinet. She shocked the doctor later with the comment, "That is a beautiful gold pen—you should never lose it. It rolled under that medical cabinet."

Therefore, near-death survivors—*and* their families and friends—should *always* appreciate how fortunate they were to survive! With quick attention and a proper combination of cardiopulmonary resuscitation, defibrillation, advanced cardiac life support, and mild therapeutic hypothermia, victims can be resuscitated successfully.

Cause of Sudden Cardiac Arrest

Please understand that sudden cardiac arrest is a specific kind of so-called "heart attack." In cardiac arrest, the heart abruptly stops pumping blood. The most common cause of cardiac arrest is an electrical problem with the heart, disrupting its pumping action. This can lead to an immediate loss of effective output of blood from the heart, circulatory arrest, and oxygen deprivation of the brain.

But a "heart attack" can also occur whenever blood is *not* reaching its intended sites. For example, the heart may still be pumping, but arteries serving the heart and brain may be blocked with cholesterol plaques.

The dismal SCAF statistics presented earlier typically result when the victim is *away* from a medical facility. He or she may have a "sudden" cardiac arrest at virtually any *other* place—home, school, office, church, or recreational site. So, even if help *seems* available, bystanders may *not* be able to respond in time or appropriately.

Cause of Near-Death Experiences

Yet, NDE skeptics and other scientists continue to claim that different medical uncertainties about a victim's condition can rationally account for his or her purported NDE "experience." Apparently, some of these "uncertainties" exist in medical settings, allowing for much conjunction. Sudden cardiac arrest

But Sam Parnia's groundbreaking 2013 book *Erasing Death: The Science That is Rewriting the Boundaries Between Life and Death* emphasizes the many clinical *nuances* that exist *not only* in restoration of the heartbeat *but also* in the assessment and management of brain functions, for improving the outcome of emergency cardiopulmonary resuscitation (CPR) for sudden cardiac arrest.

Still, however, complete recovery has been far less promising than people realize. A cascade of complicating factors can arise, particularly depending on the length of time brain anoxia occurs, before restoration of the heartbeat and oxygenated blood reaches the heart and brain. Brain cells may have initiated defensive mechanisms, for example. Recognition and proper management of these factors therefore are crucial to recovery.

As the world's leading researcher on NDE experiences, he suggests that the pathophysiology of the *sudden* cardiac arrest victim's body reveals biological processes that accompany the brain and other organs, which are well understood and are the same each time.

Reluctance to Accept

But much of the continuing dispute seems to be directed at the remarkable claims that many NDE survivors insist that they experienced. Therefore, this book will be unique from all other accounts and possible explanations you have read or heard about survivors' *real* near-death experiences.

Despite the millions of near-death experiences worldwide, academic science and the news media continue to disavow that NDEs have any spiritual revelations or implications. Their attitude may be out of respect for institutional religion, which frowns upon the reality of NDE claims.

NDE Validity

However, one researcher provided a means for distinguishing valid cases of the inexplicable "experience" that some NDE survivors do undergo. For example, survivors' reports are remarkably consistent, despite not being replicable as such by researchers. The words "as such" acknowledge that "out of body" states can be simulated with hallucinogens, for example, but can never produce the so-called NDE "core" experience.

University of Virginia professor and psychiatrist Bruce Greyson developed a 16-point scale to evaluate *claimed* near-death experiences, broken into cognitive, affective, paranormal, and transcendental components. The mean score among a large sample of *authentic* near-death experiences was 15.

NDE Memories

Moreover, Arianna Palmieri and her colleagues performed an apparently unique 2014 study about NDE survivors' *memories*. Her abstract begins with these words: "The nature of near-death-experiences (NDEs) is largely unknown but recent evidence suggests the intriguing possibility that NDEs may refer to actually 'perceived,' and stored, experiences (although not necessarily in relation to the external physical world)." The abstracts ends: "In conclusion, our findings suggest that, at a phenomenological level, NDE memories cannot be considered equivalent to imagined memories, and at a neural level, NDE memories are stored as episodic memories of events experienced in a *particular state of consciousness.*"

Eye of the Beholder

Obviously, memories of the near-death experience are no less difficult to study than the event itself. This seems true because, like the idiom "in the eye of the beholder," both the experience and its memories are unique to the survivor. Neither fits any known scientific mold, and only the survivor perceived and stored the perception.

The next chapter discusses a shocking revelation in *traditional* hypnotic psychotherapy of early *childhood* trauma.

Chapter Three

Revolution in Traditional Hypnotic Psychotherapy

Apparently Sigmund Freud was one of the early psychoanalysts to use hypnotic regression (HR) before turning to free association psychoanalysis. Nevertheless, HR had become the traditional procedure for revealing suspected *early* childhood emotional trauma. Yet, only in 1997 did Chiron and colleagues scientifically demonstrate that so-called "waking" consciousness—and its *conscious* memories—does *not* begin until the left hemisphere matures around age three. So that provided neurobiological proof that hidden traumatic memories *can* exist from *before* that age and this justified traditional hypnotic regression. A later chapter will discuss the early-maturing right hemisphere and its "hidden memories."

Of course, hypnotic regression is useful too for unearthing repressed memories of sexual abuse and PTSD. Also, hypnotic regression is now employed in our criminal justice system. Author F. J. Monaghan describes this in more detail in an online abstract from the National Criminal Justice Reference Service.

Serendipity

During the latter part of the last century, however, two eminent psychotherapists literally *stumbled upon* totally *unexpected* results while using *traditional* hypnotic psychotherapy. But the *shocking* outcomes of their two cases revolutionized hypnotic psychotherapy. This is best illustrated by the two actual case histories involving their discoveries. Both men were academically rigid and professionally trained psychotherapists—who *accidentally* gained access to *memories* never before documented in medical literature.

The credibility of their subsequent research and publications rests in consistencies in tens of thousands of individually documented case reports. However, perhaps the best proof is that *even* a medical professional using hypnotic psychotherapy may *misspeak* occasionally—as happened in the *accidental* instruction that each of these psychotherapists gave his patient during *traditional* hypnotic psychotherapy.

Past Lives

Oral traditions and written legends around the world reveal that belief in reincarnation has existed from ancient times. It was a common belief in Jesus' time. He therefore asked the disciples, "Whom do men say that I am?" referring to previous prophets being reincarnated.

Moreover, Plato (427-348 BCE) and Socrates (470-399 BCE) discussed and wrote about God-given souls, which reincarnated in different human bodies for multiple lifetimes on Earth. This meant that each immortal soul would return to Heaven upon the mortal death of each human host. Over time, therefore, each soul therefore had a series of so-called "past lives" (i.e., reincarnations), each with a different human being as host.

Yet, the idea of *accessing* memories of *souls'* "past lives" emerged only in the past thirty-five years. Probably the first psychiatrist to publicize "past-life" hypnotic regression discovered it *unintentionally* with his patient Catherine—Brian L. Weiss.

Catherine (from Weiss' first book)

"At that time, Catherine worked as a laboratory technician in a hospital where I was Chief of Psychiatry. It had taken her two months of courage-gathering to make an appointment to see me, even though she had been strongly advised to seek my help by two staff physicians, both of whom I trusted. After a few minutes [of her silence], I began inquiring … we began to unravel who she was and why she had come to see me. When we [eventually] started talking about her symptoms, she became noticeably more tense and nervous. As Catherine continued to talk, I could sense how deeply she was suffering. I decided we would begin by delving into her childhood, looking for an original source of problems. Usually this kind of insight helps to alleviate anxiety."

"She had a pediatrician good friend in the hospital to which she opened up about her life, and 'that she felt she was losing control.' He called me because he thought only I could truly understand Catherine. The Chief of Surgery also had noticed her recent unhappiness and sensed her tension. Eight weeks passed. In the crunch of my busy practice … I had forgotten about Catherine and her pediatrician friend's call."

"Eighteen months of intensive [*traditional* hypnotic regression] therapy passed, with Catherine coming to see me once or twice a week. But Catherine had not improved. On occasion, I had been successful in regressing patients back to their early childhoods, even to when they were two to three years old, thus eliciting the memories of long-forgotten traumas that were disrupting their lives. [But] her nightmares were as terrifying as ever before. I decided to regress her further [back in her childhood]. [Nothing happened, so] I instructed her firmly and clearly: 'Go back to the time from which your symptoms arise.' I was totally unprepared for what happened next. She 'flipped back' to a life thousands of years ago—*stunning* her psychiatrist!"

"However, [later] searching for documentation from my training and practice, I could find *no* clinical publications or explanation for the patient's weird response. However, after carefully reviewing her audio taped session repeatedly, I discovered that my instructions to her *might* have been *too* open-ended."

The rest is history. Miami psychiatrist Brian Weiss now has successfully *treated* thousands of patients from all walks of life. These were intractable cases whose *present-life* mental or physical problems were unresponsive to any *known* kind of treatment—other than "past-life" hypnotic psychotherapy. In other words, these had been emotionally traumatic events experienced by the *human hosts* of the patient's *soul* during *its* past reincarnations. Apparently, once the soul merges with its *current* human host, as you will read later, traumatic events from *its* past reincarnations (i.e. "past lives") may subconsciously affect its present host. These are called an "imprints."

A comment from one client's soul memory illustrates this: "Each body leaves an imprint on you (i.e., the soul) at least for awhile. There are some bodies I have had that I can never get away from altogether." Naturally, many readers may find such claims incredible. Yet, consider that our soul merges with its human host to spend an *entire* human lifetime of experiences!

Brian Weiss was reluctant about publishing his first book, *Many Lives, Many Masters: The Story of a Prominent Psychiatrist, His Young Patient, and the Past-Life Therapy That Changed Both Their Lives,* concerned about his reputation among his professional peers. Yet, it actually brought him more referrals from other mental health caregivers—a mark of respect.

Weiss wrote this at the end of that book. "Now I straddle two worlds: the phenomenal world of the five senses, represented by our bodies and physical needs; and the greater world of the nonphysical planes, represented by our souls and spirits. I know that the worlds are connected, that all is energy. My job is to connect the worlds. To carefully and scientifically document their unity."

Although Weiss has published several more recent books illustrating different aspects of past life regression therapy, one title seems to capture the overall benefit best—*Through Time Into Healing: Discovering the Power of Regression Therapy to Erase Trauma and Transform Mind, Body, and Relationships.* He writes, "I have found that about 40% of my patients need to delve into other lifetimes [of their soul] to resolve their current life clinical problems. But when past-life therapy is used to bring these long-repressed [soul] memories to awareness, improvement in the current symptoms is usually swift and dramatic."

Past Life Hypnotic Regression

So that you are *not* left wondering how past life hypnotic regression could possibly occur, Weiss offered the following description: "The process is similar to watching a movie. The present-day mind is very much aware, watching, and commenting. The mind compares the movie's characters and themes with those of the current life. The patient is the movie's observer, its critic, and its star, all at the same time. The patient is able to use his present-day knowledge of history and geography to help date and locate places and events. Throughout the 'movie' he can remain in the deeply hypnotized state."

Spiritual Hypnotic Regression

Following Brian Weiss' shocking introduction to souls' "past lives," the other psychotherapist—who discovered soul "life-between-lives" (i.e., "spiritual regression")—was caught blindsided by how it *first* happened. An academically strict professional, he had been uncomfortable with "past-life" regression. Yet, one particular patient's unusual symptoms seemed to warrant its use. Even with her family members nearby, the older woman constantly complained of being "so lonely." But California's Michael Newton had no way to be prepared for the bizarre outcome of his effort.

During the patient's trance, Newton *inadvertently* mentioned the word "group" and the patient started crying. Newton asked her why. She blurted out, "I miss some friends in my group and that's why I get so lonely on Earth." Dumbfounded, Newton asked her where her group was located. "Here, in my permanent home," she explained, "and I'm looking at all of them right now!"

Apparently, his patient was *very* hypnotizable and *mentally* had moved herself past the death scene in a past life and *into* the afterlife (i.e., Heaven). As you will read in the next section, once the host in the soul's past life dies, the soul returns to Heaven. So the patient then "became" the soul in what she said—as a soul member of her primary soul group—formed soon after all its members had just been created, developing bonds for eternity.

This was Newton's first astonishing exposure to what was then called "life-between-lives" (i.e., Heaven) hypnotic regression. But after *eventually* realizing that his patient had accidentally tapped into "this mysterious place," Newton was intrigued "to find out for myself the steps necessary to reach and unlock a subject's memory of their [soul's] existence [there]." So he dedicated a decade of research to "constructing a working model of the spirit world."

He accomplished this by developing special questioning techniques to avoid "leading the witness." But he also recognized that the overwhelming nature of the experience could cause the patient or client to mentally dawdle. Newton therefore helped subjects keep pace by asking such questions as "your impressions," "anything unusual" (i.e., about visitors, surroundings, sounds, or colors), or "other activities" (i.e., recreation, learning, or serving). Newton subsequently published ten years of research involving seven thousand cases in his first book.

Newton's first two books include many verbatim comments from his clients. These often reflect his subjects' surprise as they hypnotically relive their souls' memories of their "home of souls." Naturally, my book cannot cover their many observations about the nature of Heaven and their impressions about God—details that humans have never before been able to know.

Soul or Past-Life Host?

As you discovered, Weiss's hypnotically regressed patients reached back *before* the childhood ages typical accessed with *traditional* hypnotic regression—that had never *intentionally* been to done before. Neither did he intend that—he simply *misspoke* his instructions to Catherine. But Newton also misspoke and reached a different "stage" of soul life.

At this point in the book this may be confusing, but will be better understood later. Basically, however, we each have a God-created soul. Our soul's detailed memories of *each* of its past incarnations (or reincarnations) are accessible through special hypnotic regression. Each incarnation involves our soul's spending a human lifetime on Earth with the body, or human being (i.e., host), which each soul chooses before leaving Heaven.

When its host physically dies, the patient or client's soul returns to Heaven. The soul's memory then becomes one it has repeatedly had at the end of each of its past incarnations—its transition to and life in Heaven – as the patient or client then hypnotically perceives.

A Prelude to Spiritual Hypnotic Regression

Since some of you may have participated in a past-life regression, it is important to realize why anyone pursuing a "life-between-lives" (i.e., Heaven) regression should first *begin* with a past-life regression. This obviously accounts for the three-to-four hours required for both. But it also offers a "natural" trance progression, as follows:

As Weiss suggested in an earlier section, the patient or client visualizes a scene from one of his or her soul's past incarnations (i.e. "past lives), in which the patient/client "becomes" the human host—this is the patient/client's soul's *memory* of that earlier incarnation.
Soon, the psychotherapist guides the regression memory to and through the death scene of the human host of that incarnation. This shifts the soul memory to its leaving the death scene and its ensuing return to Heaven for the spiritual regression there – as perceived by the patient or client.

In beginning a "life-between-lives" hypnotic regression, the death scene in a hypnotized previous (soul) life is as close as possible to replicating the soul's transitional experience following *actual* physical death of its host. This then provides access to the soul's memories of Heaven.

Moreover, the past-life trance approach should be less problematic for the patient or client than an abrupt introduction to the spirit world. This also enables the subject to become comfortable first with his or her (soul's) past life, typically in just an earlier time frame.

Yet, this sequencing also affords another advantage if the past life contained unexpected trouble areas. Past-life imprints of any difficulties, such as Weiss treats, would likely go undetected if the session had proceeded directly to the spirit world. However, the psychotherapist can determine how to handle any such past-life trauma and maintain the subject's composure.

Trustworthy?

You naturally may question the trustworthiness of these patients' and clients' testimonies. However, according to Newton, "Subjects cannot lie, but they may misinterpret something seen in their *unconscious* mind just as we do in the conscious state. In hypnosis, people have trouble relating to anything they don't believe is the truth."

There have been, however, some published claims of so-called "past-lives" of *humans* that may be claimed to be trustworthy. It is therefore important to understand that human beings do *not* have previous lives. Only souls do. God creates souls in Heaven and the Divine One continues to do. Details about souls also appear later in the book. But souls are immortal, contrasted to human beings. Each soul lives forever, so to speak, and each soul incarnates in a human body for the lifetime of that person (i.e., host). Each new incarnation creates a new life on Earth for that soul—another "past life" for that soul after its host's mortal death.

Being Hypnotically Regressed

If this chapter has not shocked you, you either have been hypnotically regressed in the past or you are already familiar with what has been written about it. But before leaving this chapter, some comments are worthwhile to emphasize souls' monumental significance in human life. Our God-given souls are the closest we shall ever come to realizing the reality of the One we call God—which you will surmise from the rest of this book.

You read about Weiss and Newton's shock, and every new hypnotically regressed patient or client likely responds with great awe. The Newton Institute has trained many mental health professionals worldwide, using techniques described in Newton's third book *Life Between Lives: Hypnotherapy for Spiritual Regression*.

During the regression, you will assume two "states" of existence. One will be the person, or host, with whom your soul merged in its "past-life"; the other will be your soul in Heaven. You will be carefully guided into each by your therapist.

Reincarnation

The later chapter on reincarnation discusses the soul's commitment and preparation for reincarnation. Assume it selected your body from many that seemed to meet its objectives in this incarnation. Incidentally, it had been able to see your early life in advance. So it anticipated leaving Heaven, merging with you in your mother's womb, and sharing your life as its own.

Newton Institute

The Newton Institute's book is a collection of representative "life-between-lives" hypnotherapy cases from thirty-two psychotherapist members of the Institute around the world. That book is significant in illustrating the global unanimity of "life-between-lives" hypnotic regression results. Institute members now practice in North and South America, Europe, Asia, South Africa, and Australia. The Institute's website (newtoninstitute.org) offers a search-by-country option for finding member Institute-certified psychotherapists for the four-hour session.

An Independent Perspective

Considering what you have read thus far in this book, you likely know how science and religion feel about past-life and life-between-lives hypnotic regression. Science obviously disavows these as contrary to scientific materialism. Religions could feel that they threaten their status quo, institutional strength, and veracity of their venerated ones.

You personally may doubt the validity of patients' and clients' past-life and life-between-lives testimonies while under hypnotic regression. You therefore may be interested in a third-party commentary on Michael Newton's work. This comes from gastroenterologist Steven Hodes, who also is a teacher, author, and consultant for movies on religion and the paranormal. These excerpts were contained in his 2006 remarks on his blog "Physician to Meta-Physician: A Healing Journey" (meta-md.com) and are reproduced here with his kind permission.

Hodes acknowledges, "Michael Newton claims to have been an agnostic/skeptic about spirituality before his clinical work with superconscious hypnosis began. That is an appealing approach for me. He is not resorting to religious dogma or established theological perspectives in order to explain his findings."

He continues, "I do not expect the average reader to embrace Newtonian metaphysics at first exposure. [However,] it would be unwise to not critically explore his findings. Implications for viewing our present lives from within this continuum of multiple lives offer enormous opportunities for acceptance and transformation. Tragedy and circumstance can be seen as opportunities for growth. There is less reason to see ourselves as victims of life's random torments. If we all experience a multitude of different lives under different conditions as a variety of different religious, racial, and sexual roles, then bigotry and hatred of others becomes a waste of karmic energy. Compassion for our fellow man becomes the only reasonable attitude."

Moreover, he says, "I have been fascinated by the writings of Michael Newton since I first picked up his books. Although I initially regarded them as fantastic and even questionable metaphysical journeys--I now regard them as paradigms for ultimate healing. Yet one cannot help but be astounded by his conclusions: they are nothing less than revolutionary. They offer a picture of reality which is ultimately healing. No suffering occurs without an underlying reason and purpose. We will be with those we love for eternity."

Hodes feels, "This picture of reality is so compelling as to be 'too good to be true'. It is one of the reasons that I continue to study/ponder/ discuss and read his works. Newton is, essentially, establishing a new metaphysical/theological platform by which the mystery of existence is explained."

Without the information discussed in this book, we all still would be talking about souls in a purely philosophical-theological context. Even though theologians tacitly admit the existence of the soul, they apparently feel unwilling to openly discuss its nature and purpose. Their reluctance seems of little concern to most people, who seem to be unaware or even to deny that souls exist. God, Jahweh, and Allah—by whatever name we call The Eternal Almighty—has

Its share of attention in churches, synagogues, and mosques. But Heaven and souls apparently receive little faith, considering that death is perhaps our greatest fear.

Steven Hodes therefore expressed the following views that are more applicable in this chapter. "It [soul] is a metaphysical concept which shares a great deal with Hindu, Kabbalistic, Theosophical, mystical and some Buddhist notions of reincarnation, soul development and karma. It differs from some Eastern spiritual traditions in that Newton's patients claim that the soul retains its free will to choose its path in any particular life as well as the afterlife. If death becomes a passage way to another state of being, if love continues after death, if there truly is a higher purpose behind all of our lives, then we can more easily accept the vagaries of life as opportunities for tikkun [i.e., repair or restoration]—to heal ourselves and the world."

The next chapter introduces our God-given souls. A later chapter is devoted to details about them.

Chapter Four

What Is Our Soul?

In parts of our society, the soul is more controversial than the near-death experience. Although the term "soul" has been used in "soul food" and "soul music," there seems to be no *common* understanding of the soul as an immortal *living spiritual* entity. So even the many Amazon books about souls consider them as nebulous as the human mind.

Obviously, science disavows everything spiritual—just as they distrust anything that *cannot* be objectively proved to exist as part of their materialistic paradigm. Earlier, however, you read that a kind of *humanly* imperceptible energy *does* exist just as *real* as your Internet. That other *energy* characterizes God, souls, and Heaven. It permits their existence *without* the sustenance that humans require—air, food, and water. This freedom also enables them to exist in cosmic environments *other* than Earth. In a later chapter, you will discover the nature and appearance of a soul *as a physician/scientist describes his* from his rare NDE experience.

Philosophers have advanced theories about souls. But religious leaders make no effort to explain souls, other than the excerpt from the *Catholic Encyclopedia* included later in this chapter. Notably, the soul's relationship with God—and therefore *our* relationship with God *through our souls*—seems absent in the views of contemporary society.

Struck From Christian Theology

As you read earlier, the Eastern Roman Emperor Justinian removed souls and reincarnation from Christian doctrine. The concept of the soul therefore languished until almost a half-century ago, when it was revealed as discussed in Chapter Three. During all of that time, humans have been *unaware* of their souls. Yet, God continued creating souls in Heaven and souls continued their incarnations on Earth.

So just imagine—what if all the people around the world had known that God gave each one an immortal soul, to join him or her for a lifetime on Earth? Would we still have fallen to our dismal level of malevolence and disregard for one another? Yet, is there any *other* way in which *all* of humankind has a common bond?

Catholic Exception

But the Eternal Almighty has given each human being a soul—and He lovingly continues to do so. Probably the most cogent contemporary thought about souls still is found in the *Catholic Encyclopedia*:

"Various theories as to the nature of the soul have claimed to be reconcilable with the tenet of immortality, but it is a sure instinct that leads us to suspect every attack on the substantiality or spirituality of the soul as an assault on the belief in existence after death. The soul may be defined as the ultimate internal principle by which we think, feel, and will, and by which our bodies are animated. That our vital activities proceed from a principle capable of subsisting in itself is the thesis of the substantiality of the soul: that this principle is not itself composite, extended, corporeal, or essentially and intrinsically dependent on the body, is the doctrine of spirituality. If there be a life after death, clearly the agent or subject of our vital activities must be capable of an existence separate from the body. The belief in an animating principle in some sense distinct from the body is an almost inevitable inference from the observed facts of life."

Province of Philosophers

So the soul became the province of philosophers, beginning with the early Greek philosophers like Plato and Socrates. This continues broadly today in the concept of so-called "mind-body dualism," for which the eminent Rene Descartes' (1596-1650 CE) claimed that the mind or soul can exist without the body. Even today the so-called mind-body problem continues to confront those who seek to explain "waking" consciousness.

This therefore is to expand upon the basic principle involved in the earlier chapter—the new ability for psychotherapists to hypnotically access your and my souls' *memories* from our right cerebral hemisphere. That discussion—and its thousands of case studies around the world *validate* souls' existence in each human being.

Two points should be understood. First, past-life and "life-between-lives" (i.e., Heaven) memories are acquired and retained forever *by our souls*. This happens from their immortal series of reincarnations on Earth with human beings, with souls' pauses in Heaven between reincarnations. Second, neither the soul nor its memories are a material part of our body or our supposed "higher self." Everything about the soul is incorporeal (i.e., lacking material form or substance), just like God and the spirit world.

Therefore, as you may not realize, each God-given soul is a "work-in-progress," so to speak. As God's special immortal creation, it will have completed many reincarnations on Earth before joining your or my body, each human life with a different person—called a "host"—for that person's lifetime on Earth. When your physical body dies, your soul will return to Heaven, from which it likely will continue its series of future reincarnations.

Moreover, as you will read in a later chapter, souls' special capabilities make them *seem* more like God than like humans.

When Did God Begin Giving Each Human a Soul?

During his ten-year research interruption from professional practice to study the spirit world (i.e., Heaven), Michael Newton hypnotically regressed a woman who proved to have a "very advanced" soul. But from her, Newton discovered two special details about souls. One is included here; the other will be discussed in a later chapter.

"Almost at once," Newton wrote, "I found this woman's [soul's] span of incarnations staggering, going back into the distant past of human life on Earth. Leaping over large blocks of time [in her regression trances] I found her physical appearance changing from a slight bent to a more erect posture." From reflections she could see in pools of water, "Her sloping forehead became more vertical ... supraorbital ridges above the eyes grew less pronounced as did body hair and the massive jaws of archaic man ... I came to the conclusion [that] her [soul's] first lives [i.e., incarnations] occurred at the beginning of the last warm interglacial period which lasted from 130,000 to 70,000 years ago, before the last great Ice Age spread over the planet."

Union of Soul and Host

Michael Newton's ten years of research with life-between-lives spiritual regression concluded that the soul joins its host in the womb and the two apparently form a "relationship" that eventually shapes a single "personality" for the host. It seems intriguing to consider how a single "personality" might result. "Personality" is a totality of characteristics that form the outer "self." As such, it reflects the individual's "waking" consciousness—his or her response to how he or she perceives the world, others, and him- or herself—as well as his or her unconscious influences. These shape the person's behavior or outer self that is often called "personality."

Initially, the process of soul incarnation seems almost impossible to comprehend and therefore still is considered primarily by *experiential* evidence of its effects. It is important to keep in mind, however, that the soul is non-material (i.e., spirit or energy). Any "unification" of the soul-consciousness with the "waking" consciousness therefore is non-material too, composing two "energy" forces that hopefully will work in concert.

Yet the term "energy" can be misleading. Human understanding of energy consists of forces that conform to laws of physics and can be demonstrated. But souls are said to be individual entities of *unknown* "energy," with intelligence, imagination, intuition, and conscience vastly beyond human understanding. So please realize that *defining* the soul and soul consciousness with earth words *limits our efforts to try to understand each.* The only thing we know for sure is that transmission of information within the brain involves chemical and electrical (i.e., electromotive energy) messages. Somehow, therefore, our souls must be able to participate in determinations within our brains.

In Newton's book for mental health professionals *Life Between Lives: Hypnotherapy for Spiritual Regression,* he explains that soul incarnation is "a slow, delicate process of incredible subtlety ... begins gently, carefully following the neurotransmitters of the [fetus's] brain while matching [the soul's] own energy vibrations with the mind of the baby."

Newton acknowledges being benefited by having "medical doctors and physiologists" among his clients. He adds, "Posthypnotic suggestions have enabled [hypnotized] subjects in these professions to sketch out simplified diagrams [afterwards] of what they were trying to say about these linkages while under hypnosis."

In that book, Newton writes "Each soul has a unique immortal character ... [which] is melded with the emotional temperament, or human ego ... to produce a single but temporary personality for one lifetime. This is what is meant by the duality of our mind. With this union we are one person dealing with two internal ego (i.e., soul and human) forces inside us during life."

Why Just Recently?

So some readers may even wonder, if God began giving us souls so long ago, why is it that we have had access to soul memories through hypnotic regression *only recently*? Did God intend for us to *never* know this? Or has God helped *facilitate* our knowing *now*, for some particular reason? Remember, of course, Justinian's action in 553 CE.

In 2009, Michael Newton edited the book *Memories of the Afterlife*, a collection of case studies by members of the Newton Institute, from across the world. Many reports included his comments. The following seems to address that very matter:

"Why are the amnesia blocks about our [souls] lessening in the twenty-first century from the use of advanced methodological discoveries in hypnosis? We live in a world more overpopulated today than ever before, resulting in a diminished identity of the individual. Add to this the greatest prevalence of chemical dependence of all time. Drugs cloud the progress of the soul. Perhaps this is the reason our guides and spiritual masters are allowing more information to be released about our [human] spiritual past than ever before in human history."

The term "amnesia blocks" refers to the so-called "Veil of Forgetfulness." Souls are committed to this during each new reincarnation. Generally speaking, a soul's past lives are *consciously* forgotten *by its host* to assure that only new lessons are learned during each incarnation. The soul is committed to this, called the "Veil of Forgetfulness."

Yet, souls are immortal. Composed of spiritual (i.e., incorporeal) energy, any damage through rough incarnations can be repaired in Heaven. Although we have long been *unaware* of our souls, their amazing capabilities and non-material (i.e., incorporeal) nature have enabled them to influence many of our thoughts, decisions, and actions, but *without* our awareness. Later in the book, the creation of souls in Heaven is described by one of Newton's hypnotically regressed clients while serving as an Incubator Mother.

Do We Really Know God?

We might blame the One we call God when we don't get what we pray for or feel we deserve, or when massive calamities are not prevented from causing widespread damage, deaths, or personal hardships. But what role should we expect the Divine to play in our lives? Should we expect the Divine to control our lives – where then does free will come from, which we all have?

You learned that each human is given a soul created by God. That soul is an expression of Divine love, compassion, and benevolence. Souls also have amazing capabilities, second only to the Eternal Almighty's wisdom and power.

Yet, each soul is an individual and unique creature, with an immortal life of its own. As mentioned earlier, each can be considered a "work-in-progress," so to speak, from the time of its creation. Each has its own incorporeal life and mission for incarnations in human bodies on Earth. By the time your soul picked your body to join, that soul might have experienced hundreds of incarnations on Earth stretching over many thousands of Earth years – some of its "lives" successful and others not effective.

As each soul joins a human body to unite with its host as a *single* human personality, it has lessons to learn about how and why humans seem predisposed to moral frailties. But if the host's temperament and ego are domineering, and if the soul is weak and attracted by the host's frailties, the incarnation may have to be repeated again with similar challenges.

Yet, if the host and soul can establish a working relationship, this could foster the soul's guidance for its host - particularly on situations or in matters where the soul's prophetic awareness of the future, both visible and invisible, can guide its host. Then the soul's help actually may be more beneficial than anything the Divine might do for any human being on Earth.

In the past, all of humanity has had to depend upon their prophets and interpretations of religious scriptures for the nature of God and Heaven. But now, through the opportunity of personal spiritual hypnotic regression, anyone can learn the apparent truth about both. For those not interested in personally exploring the spirit world, Michael Newton's books are his legacy to the rest of us.

Is God Ours Alone?

Most people who believe in a Supreme Power always seem to think of the Divine as "ours." But is God involved *only* with the Earth and humans? Such thinking seems rather narrow-minded if the Divine is indeed eternal and the universe is unlimited—as NASA and cosmologists suggest. This seems to dramatically expand the magnitude of the Almighty's domain, far beyond the limited dimensions that humankind has always believed.

Furthermore, after creating everything that is, the Eternal Almighty must have also seen fit to allow species of life on Earth to modify their and their offspring's ability to survive and procreate on Earth by adapting to their changing environments. In like manner, the Divine may allow the seasons, the weather, and the seas to adjust rather than continually trying to control them.

This naturally means that we should continue our prayers of respect, admiration, and gratitude to God. Yet, the *closest* spiritual source of help in *preventing* trouble *always* will be our soul. Therefore a later chapter is entitled "Messages From Our Souls."

The next chapter helps us understand our souls from their perspective.

Chapter Five

Understanding Souls

Before soul past-life memories were *accidentally* discovered to exist in our right cerebral hemisphere, no human being even philosophers – had the vaguest idea about our God-given souls. Of course, the same was true about God and Heaven, because no human had ever physically died and returned to describe it all.

Scriptural accounts of God and Heaven often were felt to come from prophets—a later chapter about the right cerebral hemisphere, before humans developed "self-awareness," even suggests that certain of our ancestors "heard voices." But thousands of patients and clients now have been psychoanalytically documented to experience their souls' memories of its previous incarnations (i.e., reincarnations) and Heaven.

You may discount the credibility, or even disavow the possible truth, of what you are reading. Yet, no one can ever *disprove* it. Only if science, medicine, and human religions eventually acknowledge that reality *includes* both the material *and* immaterial (i.e., incorporeal) states of existence—will humankind be conscientiously free to accept the benefits granted by God.

From the Soul's Viewpoint

Researchers believe that the soul merges with the human body to create a single personality for a human lifetime. Naturally, the term "personality" means "the combination of characteristics or qualities that forms an *individual's* distinctive character." So you must be surprised—especially if you were not *aware* of your soul.

Moreover, as you will read in the later chapter devoted to souls, their special capabilities make them *seem* more like God than like humans. Therefore, this chapter is necessary so you will *not* get the wrong impression about *our* souls—yours, mine, and everybody else's—while they are with us *on Earth*.

First, our souls have emotional feelings and varied temperaments, like humans do. While in Heaven, they are among many fellow souls, where the ambience is love and peace. Yet, these comments from Newton's first book seem to apply for their reincarnations:

> "If a soul knew only love and peace, it would gain no insight and never truly appreciate the value of these positive feelings. The test of reincarnation for a soul coming to Earth is the conquering of fear in a human body. A soul grows by trying to overcome all negative emotions connected to fear through perseverance in many lifetimes, often returning to the spirit world [i.e., Heaven] bruised or hurt. Some of this negativity can be retained, even in the spirit world and may reappear in another life with a new body. [Therefore], it's in joy and unabashed pleasure that the *true* nature of an individual soul is revealed on Earth in the face of a happy human being."

But souls do *not* have *innate* weaknesses of jealousy, envy, hate, selfishness, or maliciousness. So souls expect to learn why and how we develop these moral weaknesses in life—since these are not present in human beings either—at birth or upon returning from "visiting Heaven" as an NDE survivor, as mentioned in Chapter Two.

But realize that our souls have strengths and weaknesses, as human beings do. Souls therefore *may* get *caught up* in their hosts' ego-based decisions and behavior. Naturally, many factors may govern this, including both the number and nature of our soul's reincarnation history. So, as Newton observes, "Less developed souls are inclined to surrender their will to the controlling aspects of human society, with a socio-economic structure which causes a large proportion of people to be subordinate to others."

It also seems worthwhile to reexamine the first statement in this section: "the soul merges with the human body to create a *single personality*" for its implicit meaning. Since the soul is energy, unlike the physical body, it literally might pervade the material body—not be restricted to the right cerebral hemisphere from which its past-life memories are hypnotically regressed. As this also suggests, the soul is *unlike* anything that human beings could even possibly imagine.

If so, the term "single personality" can take on a new interpretation—even as this seems suggested in the last sentence of earlier quotation. Verbatim testimonies from hypnotically regressed patients and clients use the first person singular in describing their souls' past-life experiences—each speaks as if "he" or "she" *is* the host. The word "soul" is never used! Said differently, the soul considers that *it* is experiencing life rather than its host body. But that also suggests that the soul feels responsible for decisions and actions involved, not its host.

When Newton asked one of his hypnotized regression client's soul "What is it about human hosts which might appeal to souls who are sent to earth?" the response was:

> "Those of us developing on earth have a sanction to help humans know of the infinite beyond their life and to assist them in expressing true benevolence through their passion. Having a *passion* to fight for life—that's what is so worthwhile about humanity. They can make their character mean and yet have a great capacity for kindness."

So Newton suggests, "Our eternal identity [as souls] never leaves us alone in the bodies we [souls] choose, despite our current status. In reflection, meditation, or prayer, the memories of who we really are do filter down to us [humans] in selective thought each day. In small, intuitive ways—through the cloud of amnesia [i.e., Veil of Forgetfulness]—we are given clues for the justification of our being."

Soul Influence on Human Decisions

Since we are not aware of our souls, you may wonder how our souls could influence our personal decisions and behavior without our realizing it. Perhaps it is somewhat analogous to our "autonomic" nervous system (ANS) that controls our heart and respiratory rates and visceral functions. Like our soul consciousness, our ANS is always on yet we are *not* aware of it. But the ANS is involuntary while our soul consciousness apparently is not.

The example comes to mind that, despite extensive malevolence in the world, some people *do* manifest empathy, compassion, and benevolence for others in times of great calamities. Newton seems to acknowledge this in writing: "While soul memory may be hidden from the level of conscious awareness through amnesia [i.e., veil of forgetfulness], thought patterns of the soul influence the human brain to induce motivations for certain actions."

One of the primary considerations is whether the soul and its host are well matched. In the final chapter of this book you will read that, before incarnating, each soul has the opportunity to choose its new host's family and circumstances into which to be born. Spirit world counselors are said to assist souls in their choices, which likely may involve specific challenges for further spiritual growth.

In Newton's book for mental health professionals he says: "The choice of a particular body is intended to combine a soul's character defects and strengths with certain strong and weak human emotional temperaments to produce specific trait combinations for mutual benefits." In a later chapter on souls you will discover how varied souls' innate character can be. Yet each may also acquire character modifications shaped over many previous lives on earth.

Obviously, such lifetime planning has a long time to go astray on earth. Remember that parental and other influences in early life shape subconscious memories that can affect human behavior without our awareness of the cause. Moreover, powerful instinctive human needs and desires might energetically outweigh the soul's efforts and abilities. Furthermore, unforeseen human genetic or organic mental disorders may complicate soul-body cooperation. Also, souls may succumb to human behavior that attracts their weaknesses. Hopefully, none of these or other extremes will complicate our soul's presence in our lives.

Yet, as Newton comments: "It has been said that we are never given more in life than we can handle, and to a large extent this seems to be accurate. We are who we are by design." Later in our book you will find that each of us also may receive—but not recognize—subtle messages from our soul's psychic capabilities. Examples might include knowing who is calling when the phone rings or sensing that a distant loved one was injured. You may have experienced or at least heard of something similar, called "hunches," "gut feelings," or "intuition." But soul messages seem to have different characteristics from those, since souls have a psychic perspective to which we don't have access.

Souls of Family, Friends, and Others

This may be the most shocking of what you read in this book, since each reader's focus so far has been on his or her soul. But in the later chapter on reincarnation, you will read about soul *group* reincarnation—much more common than you might even imagine. Newton's second book offers hypothetical arrangements in same or similar Earth times and geographic locations where souls in secondary groups in Heaven incarnate "together."

This may include human body choices that are relatives in one or more families, close friends, or other human relationships. Purposes for this are varied, but include possible assistance to one another [souls] on Earth. Therefore, over multiple past-lives, unusual configurations may exist within group member souls. Imagine a son in a soul's past life that shows up in its later life as a father—but *not* the same human as *both* hosts!

Sensing Your Soul

Yet, nearly everyone has "sensed" his or her soul at some time without realizing it. The best description of that is a sudden feeling "out of the blue." It usually suggests doing something different than what you were thinking, or that you customarily have done. These "feelings" often are called a "gut feeling" or "hunch" or even the more sophisticated "intuition."

For example, Malcolm Gladwell captured the public's attention with his bestseller *Blink:*

The Power of Thinking Without Thinking. It was based on the work of Professor Gerd Gigerenzer, director of the Max Planck Institute for Human Development in Berlin. Gladwell's book is filled with anecdotes in which someone's "gut feeling" proved true when confronted by cleverly faked expert opinions.

More recently, Gigerenzer wrote his own book *Gut Feelings: The Intelligence of the Unconscious.* He uses the terms "gut feeling," "hunch," and "intuition" interchangeably. He believes that these appear suddenly in our awareness *without* an apparent source or reason. He writes, "Intelligence is frequently at work without conscious thought. In fact, the cerebral cortex [i.e., of our brain] … is packed with unconscious processes."

As mentioned earlier, the *right cerebral hemisphere* matures two to three years before the left. Moreover, because of the right hemisphere's impact on our lives—usually without our awareness—it has become known as "the unconscious." The next chapter therefore discusses its significance in human life on Earth.

Chapter Six

Amazing Near-Death Experiences

Yet perhaps the most frequent occasions around the world that involve the soul are *sudden* cardiac arrests. These don't happen in health care settings, but in business, institutional, and recreational settings—requiring prompt and appropriate emergency attention.

Survivor accounts of near-death experiences attract reader curiosity. Yet, survivors once were very reluctant to tell anyone else. Now their testimonies are better accepted, however, and health care personnel increasingly accept that "something" happened. What are now called "shared-death" experiences will be discussed at the end of this chapter.

Near-Death Experiences

Just as was mentioned earlier that science still cannot explain waking consciousness in terms of the brain, skeptics of near-death experiences (NDEs) have almost exhausted their efforts to prove that these are not "real." As Dutch cardiologist Pim van Lommel and other researchers have shown, NDE survivors are convinced that their so-called "visits to Heaven" are more "real" than anything on Earth.

Therefore, before unveiling probably the classic near-death experience, it is worthwhile to review observations made by the one researcher who should know the truth. He is the world-renowned critical care and cardiopulmonary resuscitation specialist Sam Parnia. His 2013 book *Erasing Death: The Science That is Rewriting the Boundaries Between Life and Death* is a ground-breaking progress report on improving the outcome of emergency cardiopulmonary resuscitation (CPR) for sudden cardiac arrest and strengthening the chances of patient recovery.

Parnia's personal conclusions are worth noting. He feels too that so-called "near-death" victims actually have died, as suggested in Chapter Two. Further, he believes that survival of the mind or consciousness after death raises the possibility of being a new scientific phenomenon, and NDE claims are invisible to the outside world.

Beyond Skeptics' Challenges

Skeptics have advanced many purported "material" explanations for near-death experiences. Yet, since the out-of-body first stage (i.e., rising above body) seems more common than the second, it is important to acknowledge an out-of-body characteristic that *no* one has yet been able to challenge. It is the verifiable "observations" which these survivors typically claim to have made while in sudden cardiac arrest. From above the body and medical team, these include details of the resuscitation procedure; appearance of medical team members' clothing; comments made by team members; and even specific numbers on patient status monitors. Often, some of these items were even outside of the patient's view or his or her physical eyes may have been covered.

Naturally, since nearly every reported near-death experience is that survivor's *first* one, it is quite a shock for him or her. If that were you, you must realize that it would be almost impossible to "keep your wits about you" and remember everything!

Yet, one actual near-death experience did provide the survivor a vivid *recall* about literally *every* aspect of his experience. It was orthopedic surgeon Anthony Cicoria's 1994 near-death experience after being struck by lightning at an outdoor park during a family birthday gathering. The following is excerpted from his article in the July/August 2014 issue of *Missouri Medicine,* The Journal of the Missouri State Medical Association, with their kind permission:

"I ambled around the building to the pay phone and dialed my mother's familiar number, but there was no answer. With my left hand I pulled the phone hand piece away from my face to hang it up. When it was about a foot away from my face, I heard a deafening crack. Simultaneously I saw a brilliant flash of light exit the phone hand piece I was holding. A powerful bolt of lightning had struck the pavilion, traversed through the phone striking me in the face, as its massive electrical charge raced to ground.

"The force of the lightning blast threw my body backwards like a rag doll. Despite the stunning physical trauma, I realized something strange and inexplicable was happening. As my body was blown backwards, I felt 'me' move forward instead. Yet I seemed also to stand motionless and bewildered staring at the phone dangling in front of me. Nothing made sense.

"Suddenly, I realized what was going on. A motionless body was lying on the ground some ten feet behind me. To appearances the person was dead. To inspection the person resembled me. To my astonishment another look confirmed it was me! I watched as a woman who had been waiting to use the phone dropped to her knees and began CPR. I spoke to the people around my body but they could not see or hear me; but I could see and hear everything they did and said. It suddenly occurred to me that I was thinking normal thoughts, in the same mental vernacular I had always possessed. At that moment I suddenly had one simple, but ineloquent and rude thought, 'Holy shit, I'm dead.'

"This cosmic realization of consciousness meant that my self-awareness was no longer in the lifeless body on the ground. I, whatever I was now, was capable of thought and reason. Interestingly, there was no strong emotion accompanying my apparent death. I was shocked, certainly, but otherwise I felt no reaction to what should have been the most emotional of life's events. I saw no point in staying with my body, so my thoughts then moved to walk away. I turned and started to climb the stairs to where I knew my family still was.

"As I started to climb I looked down at the stairs like I would normally do. I saw that as I reached the third stair, my legs began to dissolve. I remember being disconcerted that, by the time I reached the top of the stairs, I had lost all form entirely and instead was just a ball of energy and thought. My mind was racing frantically trying to record and make sense of what was happening. Instead of bothering with the stairs, I passed through the wall into the room where everyone was. I went over to my wife who was painting children's faces. I had a clear realization that my family would be fine. Dispassionately, I departed from the building.

"Once outside, I was immersed in a bluish white light that had a shimmering appearance as if I were swimming underwater in a crystal clear stream. The sunlight was penetrating through it. The visual was accompanied by a feeling of absolute love and peace. What does the term 'absolute love and peace' mean? For example, scientists use the term absolute zero to describe a temperature at which no molecular motion exists—a singular and pure state. That was what I felt; I had fallen into a pure positive flow of energy. I could see the flow of this energy. I could see it flow through the fabric of everything. I reasoned that this energy was quantifiable. It was something measurable and palpable. As I flowed in the current of this stream, which seemed to have both velocity and direction, I saw some of the high points and low points in my life pass by, but nothing in depth. I became ecstatic at the possibility of where I was going. I was aware of every moment of this experience, conscious of every millisecond, even though I could feel that time did not exist. I remember thinking, 'This is the greatest thing that can ever happen to anyone.'

"Suddenly, I was back in my body. It was so painful. My mouth burned and my left foot felt like someone had stuck a red-hot poker through my ankle. I was still unconscious, but I could feel the woman who was doing CPR stop and kneel beside me. It seemed like minutes before I could open my eyes. I wanted to say to her, 'Thank you for helping me.' Nonsensically, all that came out was, 'It's okay, I'm a doctor.'"

No doubt you read Anthony Cicoria's experience either with your jaw dropped or in denial of its validity. Yet, he holds both MD and PhD degrees and specialty board certifications, and therefore is both a surgeon and a scientist. Moreover, he prepared his full-length article "My Near-Death Experience: A Telephone Call From God" to be a part of the July/August 2014 issue of *Missouri Medicine,* The Journal of the Missouri State Medical Association. It therefore was *not* intended for lay audiences.

His full-length article later acknowledges the multitude of such reports from around the world, as well as unsuccessful efforts from the scientific community to replicate experiences having some similarities. Yet, Cicoria concluded, "What is clear to me is that my consciousness survived death, and I was able to verify details of my near-death and out-of-body experience that I would have no conceivable way of knowing except through conscious travel of my 'spiritual self' outside of my body."

Just as Cicoria's vivid recall of *everything* he experienced is probably unique, his "physical" description of "his" eventual "state of existence" during his NDE is definitely unique: "I had lost all form entirely and instead was just a ball of energy and thought." Like all other NDE survivors, "he" was imperceptible (i.e., incorporeal) to all bystanders. Moreover, his "just a ball of energy and thought" *seems* to describe what other NDE survivors had experienced too. This idea will be examined more closely in the next chapter.

Notably, that special issue of *Missouri Medicine* was headlined "Getting Comfortable With Death & Near-Death Experiences" and was described as "[This] series will be the most encyclopedic and up-to-date in the world's literature."

However, if you search your computer for references to Anthony (Tony) Cicoria, what you will likely find is his *new* insatiable interest and ability in piano music! The word "new" means that before his sudden cardiac arrest, these did not exist for him!

An Almost Indisputable Explanation

Nearly everyone concerned with near-death experiences—scientists and the public alike—seems to overlook the one natural explanation for near-death experiences: our God-given souls! This is a real part of each of us—but this experience may illustrate how *unaware* people are of their souls!

Cicoria's NDE seems to offer, for the first time in this book and possibly anywhere, a so-called "perception" of the soul as "a ball of energy"—not a *human* perception, of course, since the soul is incorporeal (i.e., invisible) to humans!

Now compare what you have learned about souls with Anthony Cicoria's description of his first stage, out-of-body near-death experience. First, he became aware of being separated from his "dead" body—just as other cardiac arrest victims do, but "they" often simply rise above the emergency room gurney and medical team. Second, no one else could see him or hear him—he was incorporeal like souls. Third, but he felt that his so-called "spiritual self" (or "real me") came with him—as do other sudden cardiac arrest victims. Also recall the earlier claim, "NDE survivors are convinced that their so-called 'visits to Heaven' are more 'real' than anything on Earth."

NDE Survivor Perceptions

For you who are *not* familiar with perceptions that near-death survivors typically describe from their *second*-stage near-death experience, this is the stage that *includes* the so-called "visiting Heaven." The following list therefore was prepared from several sources. However, not every step is experienced with every second stage of NDE:

- Departing from the physical body;
- Viewing the physical body from an elevated position;
- Moving away and up through a "tunnel";
- Feeling peace and quiet;
- Welcoming by the overwhelming "white light";
- Sensing repair of any disabilities;
- Meeting deceased relatives, friends, and others;
- Watching a review of life to that time;
- Having a sense of ineffability;
- Being refused admittance beyond the "border"; and
- Returning to the physical body.

"Visiting Heaven"

In his first book *90 Minutes in Heaven,* Baptist minister Don Piper wrote, "I felt as if I were in another dimension. Never, even in my happiest moments, had I ever felt so fully alive. I stood speechless in front of the crowd of [deceased] loved ones, still trying to take in everything." If you are not aware, Piper had been declared dead after a dump truck crushed his small car, until a passing driver found that he was still alive.

Piper emphasized, "All of the people I encountered [in Heaven] were the same age they had been the last time I had seen them—except that all the ravages of living on earth had vanished [as had his too] ... every feature was perfect, beautiful, and wonderful to gaze at. They embraced me, and no matter which direction I looked, I saw someone I had loved or who had loved me. They surrounded me, moving around so that everyone had a chance to welcome me to Heaven."

It is noteworthy that Piper did not tell anyone about his experience for *two years,* so unbelievable did it seem to him. He spent many months undergoing reconstructive surgery and physical therapy. About two years later, the "passing driver" who finally convinced paramedics that Piper was alive—a fellow Baptist minister who was unaware that the injured man was Piper—asked Piper a question that finally disclosed his "secret."

In his second book *Heaven is Real: Lessons on Earthly Joy—What Happened After Ninety Minutes in Heaven,* Piper explains what his near-death experience meant to him as a Christian minister.

Transcendental Awareness

Kenneth Ring and Sharon Cooper's book *Mindsight: Near-Death and Out-of-Body Experiences in the Blind* seems to represent an agreement between those who differ in their theories about how NDEs and OBEs occur. This attests to the ability of blind survivors of sudden cardiac arrest to perceive the same as what sighted survivors perceive. But when one blind OBE survivor was asked the color of the medical team's clothing, she responded, "What *is* "color"?

NDE Survivor Conversions

If you are not familiar with the second stage of many near-death experiences (NDEs), the following is a review of the most-consistent outcomes from the so-called "visiting Heaven." This usual impact upon NDE survivors of sudden cardiac arrest is quite pronounced. They typically undergo a radical transformation of their attitudes about life on Earth, death, and God.

- Much greater appreciation for life itself.
- Deeper sense of wonder and gratitude about living.
- Greater self-esteem and self-confidence.
- Compassion and understanding for everyone.
- Stronger reverence for life in all of its forms.
- Disavowal of competitive and materialistic pressures.
- Caring and concern for others.
- Personal certainty about the existence of God.
- No longer fear death.

Yet, these lasting effects on the survivor often cause grave concern for his or her spouse, family, friends, and business associates—instead of inspiring awe and gratitude for the victim's survival! Obviously, their apprehension typically occurs because such alterations frequently contrast sharply with the survivor's *previous* personality and with the "normal" beliefs and behavior of those around him or her.

But psychologist Kenneth Ring comments on this in his book *Lessons From the Light: What We Can Learn from the Near-Death Experience.* He stresses "The effect of an NDE is to stimulate the growth of *self-esteem and self-acceptance, and thereby further the individual's courage to pursue a way of life in keeping with his or her own authentic self.* If we accept the truth of the NDE's chief revelation, it can only be that we have lost touch with the Source. Essentially we have fallen out of Love … and have forgotten our true home. Since Love is the essential truth of the NDE, it can also set us free.

Negative Near-Death Experiences

One of the most dramatic cases of an adult life conversion by a near-death experience was that of Howard Storm, which is described in his book *My Descent Into Death: A Second Chance At Life*. Before it happened, Storm, a professor of art at Northern Kentucky University, was *not* a very pleasant man. An avowed atheist, he was hostile to every form of religion and to those who practiced it. He would often use rage to control those around him and didn't find joy in anything. He knew with certainty that the material world was all that existed and he had no faith in anything that couldn't be seen, touched, or felt. He considered all belief systems associated with religion to be fantasies.

Then, on June 1, 1985, at the age of thirty-eight, he had a near-death experience due to a perforation of his stomach. This happened while he and his wife were on an art trip to Paris with his students. He almost did not survive.

Storm's experience was, at first, horribly gruesome, which may have reflected his worst fears. Countless creatures in a fog lured him to follow them, then began jeering and clawing at him. Terrified, he agonized, "I was alone, destroyed, yet painfully alive in that revoltingly horrible place."

Then he heard a voice saying, "Pray to God." He remembered thinking, "Why? What a stupid idea … I don't believe in God … I don't pray." Yet, a second time, then a third, he heard, "Pray to God." Then, for the first time in his adult life, a very old tune from his childhood started going through his head, "Jesus loves me…" Then, "A ray of hope began to dawn in me, a belief that there was something greater out there. For the first time in my adult life, I wanted it to be true that Jesus loved me." With all the strength he had left, he yelled, "Jesus, save me!"

Then in the darkness, a pinpoint of light appeared, like a distant star. It rapidly grew brighter and brighter, headed directly for him. He recalled, "It was indescribably brilliant; it wasn't just a light. This was a living, luminous being … surrounded by an oval of radiance."

His book described his entire experience, including his visit to Heaven and its profound impact on his life. He resigned as a professor and redirected his life by attending Union Theological Seminary. Today, he is an ordained minister, a former pastor of the Zion United Church of Christ in Cincinnati, Ohio and later a missionary to Belize. Storm's Website is http://www.howardstorm.com. His account is reproduced here with his personal permission.

From Other Cultures

A recent study among Iranian Shiite Muslims adds a significant dimension to a database developed by Jeffrey and Judy Long about the effects of near-death experiences. Jeffrey Long was one of a four-member research team headed by Alinaghi Ghasemiannejad, which reported the study results in the Fall 2014 *Journal of Near-Death Studies*. Excerpts from the abstract seem noteworthy here:

"Though an early researcher concluded that Muslim NDEs appeared to be rare, later authors concluded that they may be common and that their key features may not be very different from those of Western NDEs."

"Eight prominent features of Western NDEs were present in our participants' NDEs, and, like Western NDErs, our participants often reported profoundly positive changes in attitudes, values, and spiritual beliefs following their NDEs."

Shared-Death Experiences

In his and Paul Perry's book *Glimpses of Eternity: Sharing a Loved One's Passage from This Life to the Next,* Raymond Moody emphasized his conviction that "shared-death" experiences reveal the truth of the afterlife more than actual-death experiences. But like NDEs, these don't happen with every family. Yet, when they do, family members gathered at their loved one's bedside join him or her in a *humanly* perceptible transition of his or her soul into the afterlife. In his newest book, Moody writes,

Moody's NDE research was well known by the faculty of the Medical College of Georgia when he became a first-year medical student there. That year, a female faculty member was the first person to tell him about a "shared-death" that she experienced with her mother. "By the late 1990s, I was hearing stories of shared-death experiences from all over the world."

Moody and Perry's book contains a chapter on "Elements of the Shared-Death Experience," which describes the following aspects that often have been reported by participants.

• Geometrical changes in room's shape and a wall opening to a larger dimension.
• Indescribable mystical and brilliant light of purity, love, and peace.
• Music or musical sounds.
• Out-of-body experiences allowing participants to engage with soul's departure.
• Perception of heavenly realms of unearthly quality, serenity, and purity.
• Mist or vaporescence over the patient's body appears in a human-like shape.

Moody believes that shared empathy is the key to these events. So, if we accept that the loved one's soul is being welcomed back to Heaven by the spirit world itself, and that empathy is a characteristic of the right hemisphere, then shared-death experiences seem entirely possible— given the psychic capabilities cited in the later chapter for the souls of *both* the loved one and his or her family members.

In some cases, shared-death participants also joined their loved one in a review of his or her life, which some of them described as a panoramic view of the dying one's entire life. Interestingly, participants sometimes saw unfamiliar events in the review, which they verified later.

In his book, readers can find examples of many of these shared-death experiences among the varied reports Moody has personally received. These are from health professionals as well as lay people around the world. Moody and his family experienced such an event during the death of his mother. He wrote, "It was as though the fabric of the universe had torn and for just a moment we felt the energy of that place called Heaven."

Children's NDE Testimonies

Several NDE researchers point to the nature of young children's NDEs as *unchallengeable* evidence of the authenticity of the phenomena. *These young people describe their NDE experiences with an innocence and freshness not often found in adults. Youngsters reveal a viewpoint not yet colored by religious or societal influences. It is indeed unlikely that they have ever heard of near-death experiences.* So kids' testimonies provide a convincing baseline for the validity of NDEs that is amazingly matched by adult NDE survivors. The main difference between the two seems to be the adults' preconditioned identification of the "white light" as a familiar religious figure. Adults also may meet loved ones there who had died *without* the NDE survivor's knowledge. Children may be greeted by previously deceased siblings of whom they were *not* aware.

For example, a poignant story in the noted psychiatrist Elizabeth Kubler-Ross' book *Life After Death* involved a twelve-year-old girl. She did not share her near-death experience with her mother. The daughter had found it nicer there (i.e., Heaven) than at home and wanted to stay, but she was told she had to go back. Later, her excitement about her experience drove her to tell somebody, so she confided in her father. "What made it very special, besides the whole atmosphere and the fantastic love and light," the child said, "was that my brother was there with me and he hugged me with so much love." But after a long pause, the child complained, "The only problem is that I don't have a brother!" Her father started to cry, confessing that her brother died before she was born, and they never told her.

Melvin Morse is the best-known researcher in children's near-death experiences, having practiced his entire professional career as a pediatrician. His multiple books contain the kind of child-NDE case studies that continue to baffle health professionals just as adult NDEs do, but often with insights from children that are far beyond even adults' abilities to express.

The International Association for Near-Death Studies says, "Our research so far indicates that *about 85% of children who experience cardiac arrest have an NDE.* With improving cardiac resuscitation techniques, more and more children are surviving cardiac arrest. More children who have had NDEs are alive today, and the number is likely to increase because of improved resuscitative techniques. Apparently, youngsters of any age can have an NDE. Very young children, as soon as they are able to speak, have reported NDEs they had as infants or even in the process of being born."

The percent of children who have NDEs is more than four times the per cent of adults who do, when both have had cardiac arrests, seems to suggest that adults may have developed some sort of mental deterrent. Or perhaps children who experience NDEs simply had retained a mystical relationship with their souls, which adults have lost through the "veil of forgetfulness."

One remarkable NDE occurred while pediatrician Melvin Morse was an intern in pediatrics in a small town in Idaho. A seven-year-old named Katie had been found floating face down hours earlier in a community swimming pool. In the blunt jargon of emergency room physicians, she was a "train wreck." Miraculously, she recovered. Equally or more surprising, she told Morse that she watched her parents and brothers in their home, apparently before they had been notified. Morse described what she did:

"Katie wandered through her home, watching her brothers and sisters play with their toys in their rooms. One of her brothers was playing with a GI Joe, pushing him around the room in a jeep. One of her sisters was combing the hair of a Barbie doll and singing a popular rock song. Katie drifted into the kitchen and watched her mother preparing a meal of roast chicken and rice. Then she looked into the living room and saw her father sitting on the couch. Later, when Katie mentioned this to her parents, she shocked them with her vivid details about the clothing they were wearing, their positions in the house, and even the food her mother was cooking." This was reproduced from Melvin Morse's 1991 book with his kind permission.

Regarding children's near-death experiences, Kenneth Ring believed that these children's stories seem to be describing something that is *intrinsic* to the human personality once it is caused to enter the state of consciousness that ensues on coming close to death. Ring also revealed several less-publicized changes that happen to some child NDE survivors. He feels that the NDE unleashes normally dormant potentials for *higher consciousness* and extraordinary human functioning:

•They experience states of expanded mental awareness … flooded with information;
• It seems to accelerate the development of … psychic sensitivities; and
•There is a strong connection with the development of healing gifts afterwards.

The next chapter continues *real* experiences involving young children, which may seem as incredible as their near-death experiences.

Chapter Seven

The Magic Time

This chapter is dedicated to children. However it's not for them. It's for us adults—about them. Unless you've been around a very young child recently, you may not remember what they can be like: fresh, innocent, spontaneous, loving, honest, and inquiring. The verb "can be " is used to emphasize that these traits are free-flowing ones that naturally emerge when fetuses and babies are "secure," surrounded by love and nurturing.

However, as the chapter quotation suggests, once youngsters become concerned about survival—and later about materialism and success—their innocence can start to fade. Remember that souls offer humans a "transcendent source of consciousness" until the "veil of forgetfulness" descends. Also, that it may be the developing ego of the child that eventually helps draw the curtain. But before this occurs—apparently sometimes as late as early school years—some children exhibit apparent metaphysical abilities. Even though these apparently are manifested by their soul consciousness, these children consider them "normal."

Naturally we parents are far removed from our own passage through those early years. So we typically will criticize anything like premonitions or invisible playmates from our children. Part of this is due to disbelief and part is protectionism: "What would our friends and neighbors think?" Fortunately, a few, more-tolerant parents listened, watched, and carefully documented their children's revelations. This chapter provides accounts of a few of those children and their experiences, taken from various sources.

Marcus Borg

Marcus Borg's book *The Heart of Christianity: Rediscovering a Life of Faith* contains a story that illustrates the preceding points. It involves a three-year-old girl who excitedly asked to speak to her newborn brother as soon as he came home from the hospital. But she wanted to do so behind a closed nursery door. The parents were naturally apprehensive but were able to listen in on an intercom and intercede if necessary. Soon they heard her say to him, "Tell me about God—I've almost forgotten."

Borg adds, "This story is both haunting and evocative, for it suggests that we come from God, and that when we are very young, we still remember this, still know this. But the process of growing up, of learning about *this* world, is a process of increasingly forgetting the one from whom we came and in whom we live. The birth and intensification of self-consciousness, of self-awareness, involves a separation from God. The world of the child, with its mystery and magic, is left farther and father behind."

Saved From Widow Syndrome

A seventy-one year old woman felt she had escaped the "widow syndrome"—a condition in which a woman often dies from despair shortly after the death of her husband—because of her ten-year-old niece. The girl had been terminally ill with cancer, so sick that she could not lift her head. Yet a short time before she died she sat bolt upright in bed and told her mother, "You can't go with me! The light is coming to get me but you can't go! I wish you could see it. It's so beautiful." Later, the niece's remarks about the afterlife reassured her aunt, after her husband's death.

Linda's Son

Linda's son came to breakfast, looking tired. He said he'd had a very vivid dream. A tall lady in white "like a glowing princess" had told him that time was running short. All the doors around him in the dream closed and the only place left to go was down a long hallway. "It was weird," he said. He continued to have that dream and drew pictures of things in the dream. Later during a walk he took his mother's hand and said in a most serious tone, "If I die, don't cry about it. I know I'm going to be happy there because they showed me. It's beautiful." Two days later he was accidentally shot in the chest at a party. Someone had found a loaded gun and passed it around. It accidentally discharged with him holding the barrel. His parents found a tall monument on a nearby gravesite and a tree at his gravesite, exactly as he showed on his drawing.

Carol Bowman

One day Carol Bowman's young children shocked her. Her daughter recalled dying long ago in a house fire and her son told a story about dying during a Civil War battle. At the time Bowman had no notion about "past lives." But her young kids' descriptions were so vivid and graphic that she wondered where they could possibly have acquired their ideas. Days later it dawned on her that her children's recollections had enabled them to let go of their previous fears about fire and loud noises. Confused, she searched in vain for reports of similar experiences with other children. Finding only a scholarly work by Ian Stevenson, she decided to do her own research. She got a graduate degree in counseling and began accumulating cases on her own. Parents started seeking her out to ask about odd experiences with their own children. She has written two books documenting many cases, *Children's Past Lives: How Past Life Memories Affect Your Child* and *Return from Heaven: Beloved Relatives Reincarnated Within Your Family.*

Tobin Hart

Tobin Hart, professor of psychology at West Georgia University, had an unusual experience with his youngest daughter that prompted him to embark on fascinating research. While bidding her good night one evening, she quietly asked him, "Daddy, do you see the pretty lady?" He fortunately said no, but asked, "Would you tell me about her?" The outcome years later was his seminal book *The Secret Spiritual World of Children: The Breakthrough Discovery that Profoundly Alters Our Conventional View of Children's Mystical Experiences* and his founding of the Child Spirit Institute (http://childspirit.org).

James Peterson

Elementary school teacher James Peterson had a unique experience as a camp counselor that led him on a seventeen-year exploration of the psychic world of children. The incident happened during a break in the camp schedule when the kids were in the swimming pool and Peterson relaxed in meditation in the bunkhouse. His rest was interrupted, his eyes still closed, to find eight-year-old Drew and nine-year-old Eric watching him intently. As Peterson kept his eyes closed, he heard one whisper, "Do you see what I see?" The other replied, "Yeah, it's weird." Peterson wrote, "Then they began to describe to each other swatches of color they saw floating around various portions of my body" (i.e., aura). This became part of his master's degree project at the University of California at Berkeley, published later as "Some Profiles of Non-Ordinary Perceptions of Children." His work culminated in his book *The Secret Life of Kids: An Exploration Into Their Psychic Senses.*

Schoolteacher Peterson's book singles out one seventh-grader named Jenny Ann in the school where he taught for her "clear, full-color" precognitive visions. Jenny Ann described them, "It's not fuzzy or anything, and it lasts for only a split second. It's usually a picture of someone doing something. The events I see are not big things, just little things. Then a few days later, I'll see the same event happening in real life." As she aged, the frequency of her visions diminished, which seems characteristic of these youngsters.

Derek

Six-year-old Derek was dying of a type of tumor called a "neuroblastoma," or at least that's what the doctors thought. He had been in the hospital for several weeks, and his rapid deterioration indicated a very grim prognosis. At best, Derek was expected to live only about a month longer. But he had an entirely different notion of what would happen. One day, he drew a picture of himself in which the tumor had disappeared. He told his doctor that he'd had a vision the night before in which the tumor left his body. Although his doctor insisted it was merely a dream, Derek claimed it was much more than that. He said it was real. He proved to be right. From that day on, the boy improved until he had a complete remission.

Becky

Becky's physician told her that chemotherapy had worked and she would survive her brain tumor. All their high-tech medical tests proved it. That night, Becky had a vision in which a woman told her that she was going to die. Her doctor insisted it was only a dream. But Becky maintained that she knew it was real. She said the vision was as clear as though people had come into the room and spoken to her. Within weeks her condition deteriorated and she died.

Jenny

A seven-year old girl named Jenny was riding in the backseat of her family car when suddenly she asked, "Mommy, if a man in a big truck, a man who can't speak English, bangs into our car and doesn't hurt us but smashes the car, do we have to pay to get the car fixed?" What an odd question her mother thought, and then explained how insurance worked. A few minutes later their car was hit by a dump truck, driven by a man who couldn't speak English. Though no one appeared hurt, Jenny was hysterical and was taken to the hospital for examination, during which she blurted out tearfully to the physician "It was my fault!" Asked what was her fault, she said, "I knew the accident was going to happen and I didn't tell Mommy."

Eryl Mai

On Friday, October 21, 1966, a mountain of coal waste, perched above the Welsh mining village of Aberfan, broke loose and came flowing down uncontrollably. De-stabilized by recent rains, a river of black coal sludge, water and boulders bore down on Aberfan. It steamrollered over a tiny cottage halfway down the slope, thundered through Pantglas Junior School, obliterated a further twenty houses, then finally came to rest. A total of 144 people, including many children, were crushed or suffocated to death in one of Britain's most horrific peacetime tragedies. Every life lost was precious. But the death of 116 innocent children, killed in the school, tore at the very heart of the nation. In a cruel irony, the youngsters had been making their way back to their classrooms when the disaster struck, after singing *All Things Bright and Beautiful* at morning assembly.

No one in that close-knit community was unaffected by the tragedy and the bereaved parents would never recover from their loss. But for one family, the overriding grief was even more acute. One of those killed, ten-year-old Eryl Mai Jones, had not only predicted the catastrophe, but had warned her mother of it, too.

In the days leading up to the atrocity, Eryl had told her mother she was "not afraid to die. I shall be with Peter and June," she added. Eryl's busy mother offered her imaginative daughter a lollipop and thought no more about it. Then, on October 20, the day before the disaster, Eryl said to her mother: "Let me tell you about my dream last night. I dreamt I went to school and there was no school there. Something black had come down all over it!" The next day, Eryl's horrific premonition came to pass and she was killed alongside school friends Peter and June. They were buried side-by-side in a mass grave, just as the youngster had predicted. Susan Chalmers covered this story in her online article "Yes, We Do Have a Sixth Sense: The In-Depth Study of Our Intriguing Dreams That Convinced One Doctor."

Mattie Stepanek

Mattie died at fourteen from a rare disease, after his full life of helping people acquire empathy. He was frequently seen on The Oprah Show in his wheelchair and attached to tubes that kept him alive, talkative, and upbeat. His mother, Jeni, said that, from a very early age, Mattie felt that "his purpose for being of earth was to be a messenger, to make people smile despite challenges."

Humans Don't Have Colors

Even school periodicals have documented kids' apparent psychic prowess, as evidenced by an article in the September 1974 issue of *Teachers* magazine. This was cited in Chamberlain's 2013 book: "Two- to six-year-old children who haven't been taught better nearly always draw human figures who are surrounded by colors. However, when their teachers point out that humans do not have any colors around them, the children obediently quit drawing the auras."

Personal

For this final example let me admit my own ineptitude in failing to recognize our own grandson's apparent transcendent sense in a question he asked me when he was five, when I was still a skeptic. His question was: "Granddaddy, what if this is not the *real* world?" A most innocent question, but one he obviously was very serious about. I failed miserably. I remember asking him if he meant something like dreaming. But it must have been obvious to him that I had no idea what he was talking about. So he dropped the matter and I missed a golden moment. But each time I blame myself for that, I recall Saint Thomas Aquinas' words, "For those with faith, no explanation is necessary. For those without, no explanation is possible." As with most of these children, our grandson had forgotten the incident years later.

Don't React

If you've never encountered or heard of an occasion such as these, either the parents wouldn't admit it or it is because many children don't manifest such behavior. For those children who do, however, they themselves don't consider it abnormal. Parents who are willing to listen without reacting negatively therefore should respond to the experience simply as they would to any other observation by their children. To caution the child unduly can attach some special significance to it in his or her mind. In time, he or she will learn that friends consider it weird.

We might wonder how these situations are possible. *One conceivable speculation is that the child's soul-consciousness is more mature and perhaps more capable of bringing its awareness to the child before the child's "veil of forgetfulness" descends.*

Chapter Eight

Our Unappreciated Right Cerebral Hemisphere

Despite the fact that God has given everyone a unique soul, and will continue to do so forever, the significance of our *right hemisphere* as the source of *soul memories* has been revealed only recently, as discussed in Chapter Three. So this chapter discusses other aspects of the right hemisphere that account for its *unconscious* influence.

Naturally, you are well aware of your so-called "waking" consciousness and the conscious memories it provides. With it, you are fully "aware" of everything that happens to you and around you, plus a variety of information, thoughts, questions, decisions, and the like. This naturally includes what you see, hear, touch, smell, and taste.

However, this chapter will surprise you with memories of which you are *not* aware—that come from *other* forms of "consciousness" of which you also are *not* aware. One is discussed in this chapter; a second is discussed in a later chapter.

Yet, there were historic origins for these claims a century or more ago. One was in the eminent William James' 1902 book *Varieties of Religious Experience*. He wrote, "Our normal waking consciousness ... is but one special type of consciousness, whilst all about it, parted from it by the filmiest of screens, there lie potential forms of consciousness entirely different."

James was a physician, philosopher, and psychologist, and he was the first educator to offer a psychology course in the United States.

One Different Form of Consciousness

There is a ubiquitous *inability* of human beings to consciously recall anything from our very early childhood. For most people, it is *not* until *after* they were two to three years of age, or even later. As you learned earlier, Chiron and colleagues scientifically demonstrated that "waking" consciousness—and its conscious memories—does not begin until the left hemisphere matures around age three. Although the following details may seem complicated, these help us realize the nature and sophistication of our brain's operation—and the remarkable significance of the right hemisphere in our entire lives.

Revelations About Our Brain

Neuroscience has opened a so-called "Pandora's Box" to challenge our modern assumptions about human consciousness—the part of us with which we felt so comfortable. Never mind that the eminent David Chalmers still insists that consciousness is "the hard problem." Yet, neuroscientist David Eagleman helps *dismiss* the significance of our *personal* consciousness by supporting scientifically documented human capabilities that may involve our *unconscious* right hemisphere.

One is that decisions are *unconsciously* made 7-10 seconds *before* they are consciously known, according to Max-Planck-Gesellschaft's "Unconscious Decisions in the Brain." The second is that a future event is *unconsciously* known (i.e., precognition) through physiological changes, detected in cardiopulmonary, skin, and/or nervous systems, as described by Julia Mossberg, et al. "Predicting the Unpredictable: Critical Analysis and Practical Implications of Predictive Anticipatory Activity."

Eagleman's two books, *Incognito: The Secret Lives of the Brain* (2012) and *The Brain: The Story of You* (2017), are written for the lay public. So they are both informative and entertaining—if you are willing to have your beliefs challenged. But many scientific authorities have demonstrated that this is how we can keep our brains healthy and growing, regardless of our age, because of cerebral plasticity.

Since these two seeming paradoxes apparently do occur, we might wonder whether the right hemisphere accounts for other phenomena that science's materialism paradigm would disallow. For example, remote viewing, after-death communications, and extrasensory perception, seem to have been documented—as well as near-death experiences.

Also, it is *not* beyond wondering whether the human soul residing there is involved in any way, with its unique capabilities. Yet, with the soul's nature of incorporeal energy, any research involving the soul seems beyond even neuroscience's capabilities.

Hemisphere Anatomy

The largest part of our brain, at the top of our head, is called the "cerebrum." It is associated with higher brain functions, such as thought and action, and is divided into two, side-by-side vertical halves called "hemispheres."

Although equal in size, the two hemispheres have mostly different functions. Each hemisphere is covered with a dense folded outer layer packed with nerve cells. Together, these twin layers form the cerebral cortex (i.e., two cortices). A bundle of nerves at their bottom rear, called the "corpus callosum," connects them. Its purpose is to keep each one's characteristic functions from being duplicated by the other one.

The cortex has been called the most important part of our brain, especially for psychology, because it is what makes us human. It is packed with neurons (i.e., nerve cells) at birth, which makes early infancy so crucial in shaping a human being's *entire* life.

Across the two hemispheres (i.e., cortices) the frequency (i.e., operations) of their functions differs according to the person's state of activity. The frequency can be measured on a device called an "electroencephalogram" (EEG). Technically, the left hemisphere operates at a faster frequency (i.e., beta waves) than the right, consistent with our busy daily lives and waking consciousness. However, the right hemisphere has three different frequencies (i.e., alpha, theta, and delta, in that order), slowing according to our state of mental activity: relaxed or meditative, hypnosis, and sleep.

But realize that this description is very simplistic, only to illustrate general cortex operations—the range from "full" left to "full" right hemisphere is very broad and change is very subtle.

Memories

The left hemisphere brings brain faculties that make possible the many mental processes you use daily. The left hemisphere therefore becomes the dominant half in later years, apparently because of the fast pace of our lives with left hemisphere functions.

But the adjacent half of your cerebrum—called your "*right* hemisphere"—becomes active at birth and is therefore dominant until two to three years of age. So just as you formed *conscious* memories after that, you formed *unconscious* memories before that age. Both kinds of memories are created from your emotional experiences, but the ones before ages two to three remain "hidden" (i.e., consciously inaccessible).

Yet, if any of those earlier *experiences* were *very* emotional—fear of being left alone or feelings of not being loved, for example—those "hidden" memories also included *how you reacted* at *that t*ime. Yet, unless resolved, negative "hidden memories" can resurface *without your awareness* throughout life. This may cause you to behave adversely, typically in interactions with other people or even about "things"—mimicking the emotional reaction imprinted with your original experience.

Addressing Hidden Memories

UCLA clinical professor of psychiatry Daniel Siegel explains the connection between "implicit [i.e. hidden] memories" and "awareness" in his book *Mindsight: The New Science of Personal Transformation*. He says that recent discoveries help us understand how implicit memory can influence our present lives without our realizing that something from our past is affecting us. This is of special significance when you understand that your *conscious* memories represent only a small fraction of "memories" stored within you.

Significance of Right Cerebral Hemisphere

In 2008, John Bargh and Ezequiel Morsella published a research summary of forty-eight scientific publications about "the unconscious" (i.e., right hemisphere). This confirmed that the neurobiological template for infant development (i.e., differential timing of hemisphere maturity) "permits cultural guides to appropriate behavior to be 'downloaded' during early childhood development. It greatly reduces the *unpredictability* of the child's world and his or her *uncertainty* as to how to act and behave in it."

Our Remarkable Right Hemisphere

Moreover, from your right hemisphere, your soul has a very different perspective of life than your left hemisphere does—from spiritual as well as material standpoints. Although your soul keeps you from *consciously* knowing *its* past lives (i.e., "Veil of Forgetfulness"), its other capabilities are *not* blocked. In addition to two of its possible influences at the end of this chapter, your soul has senses that reach far beyond our five human physical senses! This can be very important if you "don't know the road ahead," so to speak. Therefore, your soul often is able to influence your thoughts, feelings, concerns, decisions, intentions, and plans—without your knowing.

Functional Differences Between Hemispheres

Throughout our lives, our right and left cerebral hemispheres have different functions and perspectives about life. For example, the right is holistic, subjective, and intuitive, while the left is focused, objective, and rational. Capabilities of the soul's right hemisphere *consciousness* are only *now* becoming realized by science. This seems especially true when the right hemisphere's "unknown" is contrasted to the left hemisphere's "waking" consciousness.

Nor do the two hemispheres share a common "language," according to neuropsychologist Rhawn Joseph. In his publication, "Right Brain Unconscious Awareness," he offers many right hemisphere characteristics that might serve the soul well. For example, each half of the brain is concerned with, perceives, analyzes, and memorizes different kinds of information. So emotionally traumatic memories can be triggered in the right hemisphere but be ignored by the logical left hemisphere. Moreover, the left hemisphere may not relinquish its control over behavior. Some left-brains may even pride themselves on being rational.

This could dampen soul influence on the human being, since some left-brains do not believe in intuition or gut feelings, discussed earlier. Therefore, from a *conscious* perspective, much of what occurs in the domain of the right hemisphere is not subject to scrutiny or analysis by the left hemisphere, since the latter cannot recognize it verbally.

Moreover, British psychiatrist Ian McGilchrist warns, "with the advent of electronic platforms, we communicate in 'written' language *far more* than ever before." Our left cerebral hemisphere increasingly dominates our relationships with typically impersonal, often coded, and sometimes incomprehensible "text" messages.

Lifetime Hemisphere Differences

In clinical neuropsychologist Allan Schore's 2010 publication entitled "The Right Brain Implicit Self," Schore writes, "It is the right hemisphere and its implicit [i.e., unconscious] functions … that are truly dominant in human existence. Over the lifespan, the early-forming unconscious implicit self [i.e., right hemisphere] continues to develop to more complexity, and it operates in qualitatively different ways from the later-forming conscious explicit self [i.e., left hemisphere]." He also wrote, "The unconscious represents the inner world described by psychoanalysis since its inception."

For clinicians only: The expanded and enhanced view of "the unconscious" in *social psychology* is more compatible with theory and evidence in the field of evolutionary biology than is the "subliminal only" view of *cognitive psychology*.

Roles of the Unconscious

In Baylor College of Medicine neuroscientist David Eagleman's book *Incognito: The Secret Lives of the Brain*, he writes, "The first thing we learn from studying our own [brain] circuitry is a simple lesson: most of what we do and think and feel is *not* under our conscious control. Brains are in the business of gathering information and steering behavior appropriately." Eagleman should know—he is director of Baylor's Laboratory for Perception and Action.

He suggests that "feeling" states of the body can "provide hunches that can steer behavior." Furthermore, "These hunches turn out to be correct more often than chance would predict, mostly because your *unconscious* brain is picking up on things first, and your consciousness lags behind."

His fascinating book tracks the history of people and experiences that, over time, helped advance this awareness. In Eagleman's concluding words, "We're now getting the first glimpses of the vastness of inner space."

Self-Awareness

Infants before a certain age are familiar with their own bodies, but are *not* aware that others are individuals as they are, until they become older. Remember that our right and left cerebral hemispheres mature at a different rate. Although so-called "waking" consciousness comes with the left hemisphere two to three years after birth, self-awareness does not seem related to that. Of course, the right hemisphere that is again discussed in the next section apparently is active at birth. But, in the context of human brain evolution, humankind apparently has *not* always been "self-aware."

Perhaps one of the examples of this was the Biblical account of Adam and Eve in the Garden of Eden. It tells of their eating fruit from the Tree of Knowledge. In doing so, they became aware (i.e. "self-aware" or self-conscious) and realized that they were naked.

Historical Significance of the Right Hemisphere

Julian Jaynes probably was the most respected psychologist, researcher, and scholar in the historical underpinnings of the significance of the right cerebral hemisphere. The following is reproduced from his paper "Consciousness and the Voices of the Mind" at the 1983 McMaster-Bauer Symposium on Consciousness, with the kind permission of the Julian Jaynes Society, Henderson, NV:

> "At the time that I was thinking in this primitive fashion [i.e., bicameral mind], in the early 1960s, there was little interest in the right hemisphere. Even as late as 1964, some leading neuroscientists were saying that the right hemisphere did nothing, suggesting it was like a spare tire. But since then we have seen an explosion of findings about right hemisphere function, leading, I am afraid, to a population that verges on some of the shrill excesses of similar discussions of asymmetrical hemisphere function in the latter part of the 19th century and also in the 20th century.
>
> "What I have tried to present to you is a long and complicated story. It leaves us with a different view of human nature. It suggests that what civilized us all is a mentality that we no longer have [i.e., a lack of self-awareness] in which we heard voices called gods. Remnants of this are all around us in our own lives, in our present-day religions and needs for religion, in the hallucinations heard particularly in psychosis, in our search for certainty, in our problems of identity. And we are still in the arduous process of adjusting to our new mentality [i.e., self-awareness] of consciousness. The final thought I will close with is that all of this that is most human about us, this [i.e., self-awareness] consciousness, this artificial space we imagine in other people and in ourselves, this living within our reminiscences, plans, and imaginings, all of this is indeed only 3,000 years old."

The term "bicameral" means "two-chambered" (i.e. cerebral hemispheres). One part had seemed to speak and the other part to listen and obey, assuming each hemisphere operated separately back then. But you learned earlier that humans always have had souls. So, before self-awareness, were we more accessible to hearing from the Divine through our soul? Recall Judean Old Testament accounts, that may otherwise be considered fictitious?

The British Journal for the History of Philosophy and other notable historic references suggest that Socrates may have supported Jaynes' theory. That Socrates took himself to possess a divine sign is well attested by ancient sources. Both Plato and Xenophon mention Socrates' *daimonion* on numerous occasions. What is problematic for contemporary scholars is that Socrates unfailingly obeyed the warnings of his sign. Scholars have worried that Socrates seems to ascribe greater epistemic authority to his sign than his own critical reasoning.

Moreover, he never so much as questioned the authority of his sign to guide his actions, much less its divine nature. So Socrates questioned the authority of many of the Athenian gods and claimed to be guided by his inner daimonion. He was charged with impiety, which was entirely acceptable in a democracy reverential to their gods. It led to his death sentence.

Jaynes' theory was supposedly in keeping with the evolution of the brain. Perhaps our development of self-awareness inculcated in us a trait previously missing, one whose absence had fostered earlier communal living in small groups. If self-awareness developed, as did so-called "civilization," was self-awareness responsible for our becoming individually selfish?

Another perspective helps support Jaynes' theory. The eminent practicing psychiatrist and psychoanalyst, Elio Frattaroli, criticizes his mental health colleagues for their dependence on prescription medicines. His book *Healing the Soul in the Age of the Brain: Becoming Conscious in an Unconscious World* stresses "why listening to the soul is the key to becoming the full, rich person we each have it in us to be."

Notably, he explains: "Unlike Plato and the many religious teachers who had located the soul in our inner sense of morality, Descartes discovered it in the simple but profound experiencing of self-awareness. We now take as self-evident the distinction between the private inner world of introspective awareness [i.e., self-awareness] and the public outer world of sensory awareness (including the awareness of our own bodies), but in fact it is only since Descartes that we have become able to recognize this distinction."

As a psychoanalyst, Frattaroli continues: "We define ourselves no longer in terms of what we [once] felt, but what we [now] think and perceive, instead of dealing in a meaningful way with human emotions, and still less with the experience of inner conflict. We no longer recognize the 'existential emotions' of anxiety, shame, and guilt as signals of moral conflict, central to the life of the soul. We prefer not to think about those experiences that later caused our innermost emotions of anxiety, guilt, or shame. Yet, by doing so (i.e., learn from those experiences) we begin to know ourselves. This enables us to recognize the setting of our actions at that [earlier] time, as well as to help heal any emotional turmoil they caused us in retrospect."

Kids' "Prior-Life" Memories

In contrast to the general imposition of the "Veil of Forgetfulness," some young children have been documented to *accurately* describe their *soul's* memories about "their previous" life and death—recall the young child who became known for "his" memory as a WWII fighter pilot?

Often, some kids spontaneously have claimed being mistreated, such as the wrong breakfast foods or clothing different from what they *used* to eat and wear. Apparently, they remembered the life and death of their *soul's* human host from its previous reincarnation. That may have occurred far away, even in a different culture.

This intrigued University of Virginia psychiatrist Ian Stevenson (1918-2007) so much that he spent forty years—sometimes traveling 55,000 miles a year—to investigate and assiduously detail 2500 such cases around the world. He was able to objectively *validate* 1200 of these. Researchers have shown that such spontaneous recall of soul past-life memories usually fade as the child ages.

An Unusual Imprint

Yet such *immediate* past-life soul recall among the very young may also suggest why an *unconscious* (i.e., "hidden") memory of the *previous incarnation* of an individual's *soul* may become a serious problem for growing youngsters. This was revealed in an extensive online article "Dr. Ian Stevenson's Reincarnation Research." It says, "Often children [i.e., boys] who were members of the opposite sex [i.e., girls] in their [soul's] *previous* life show difficulty in adjusting to their new [male] gender. In other words, former girls who were reborn as boys may wish to dress as girls or prefer to play with girls rather than boys." The complete online reference is in the Bibliography.

Since our so-called "mind" has yet to be defined for its possible role in right hemisphere "unconscious" phenomena, it is the subject of the next chapter.

Chapter Nine

The Human Mind

Most scientists likely will disavow the possibility that our mind could be involved in near-death experiences. Yet, the discovery of our soul offers new possibilities of its unknown capabilities.

An online article from *Psychology Today* entitled "What Is the Mind? Understanding Mind and Consciousness via the 'Unified Theory'" is especially pertinent to this discussion. Its author, Gregg Henriques, is a professor of psychology at James Madison University. He writes, "We need to first get clear about what most folks mean when they use the term "mind."

What, exactly, are they referring to? In common parlance, 'the mind' most often refers to the seat of human consciousness, the thinking-feeling 'I' that seems to be an agentic causal agent that is somehow related but is also seemingly separable from the body.

The idea of life after death is so intuitively plausible to so many because our mental life seems so different from our bodies that we could imagine our souls existing long after our bodies decompose. This leads to a common sense dualism that is part and parcel to many religious worldviews."

However, "the Unified Theory suggests there are some semantic problems referring to the human self-consciousness system as 'the mind.' One reason why has to do with what Freud discovered over a century ago (i.e., the 'unconscious') and is now well known by modern day psychologists. Consciousness is only a small portion of mental processes. *Conscious* memories represent only a small fraction of "memories" stored within you. Consciousness and mind are thus not synonymous."

Furthermore, the legendary Canadian neurosurgeon, Wilder Penfield, who was able to make maps of the brain on awake patients (i.e., brain has no pain fibers) to track motor cortices with skeletal muscles, constantly searched for the mind. In his last book, *Mystery of the Mind: A Critical Study of Consciousness and the Human Brain,* he wrote:

"It is clear that, in order to survive death, the mind must establish a connection with a source of energy other than that of the brain. If during life (as some people claim) direct communication is sometimes established with the minds of other men or with the mind of God, then it is clear that energy from without can reach a man's mind. In that case, it is not unreasonable for him to hope that after death the mind may waken to another source of energy."

According to Valerie Hunt's seminal book *Infinite Mind: Science of the Human Vibrations of Consciousness,* two other eminent neurophysiologists, John Eccles and Ragnor Granit, agreed with Penfield, "There is nothing in the brain to account for the high level of experiences and capabilities of the mind. They further qualified these higher capabilities as intuition, insight, creativity, imagination, understanding, thought, reasoning, intent, decision, knowing, will, spirit, or soul."

At that time, of course, neither Brian Weiss nor Michael Newton had stumbled upon hypnotic regression access to everyone's soul memories from their right cerebral hemisphere. But Newton later characterized soul attributes as "an apparently unlimited and unexcelled consciousness with insight, conscience, imagination, honesty, intuition, intelligence, special senses beyond human comprehension, and creativity far beyond anything on Earth."

Furthermore, the new book by neuroscientist John Dowling, *Understanding the Brain: From Cells to Behavior to Cognition,* was published twenty years after his earlier book, *Creating the Mind: How the Brain Works.* The Amazon review said of his earlier book said, "Over the past century, our understanding of the brain has raced forward to reveal many of the mechanisms by which the brain creates mind and consciousness." But the Ars Technica's review of Dowling's newest book said, "Yet our understanding of the mind has not exploded apace with our understanding of the brain—scientists and philosophers can't even agree on a definition of what the "mind" is.

So just *what* was *that* extra "something" that separated *with* the soul during near-death experiences? Cicoria called it his "spiritual self"—and other survivors call "it" "the real me"? This chapter therefore explored the continuing enigma of our mind as possibly being one of our soul's many God-given capabilities.

Yet, it obviously is untenable for this book to even suggest that the soul constitutes the human mind and that *it* is what separates with the soul at death—despite its possible truth. Judge for yourself.

The next chapter therefore offers a more plausible conclusion about our souls' possible involvement in near-death experiences.

Chapter Ten

The Soul as the Key to Near-Death Experiences

Remember Newton's claim, "The soul merges with the human body to create a *single personality* for that host." So consider that, during each incarnation into a human body, the soul spends the same *human* lifetime on Earth as its host—and it shares each and every experience of its host. Each and every thought, question, intention, decision, action, and memory is *shared* between soul and host—despite the host's probable lack of awareness. The soul's memory also includes those so-called "hidden memories" before "waking" consciousness arrived for its host. Furthermore, the soul knows everything that occurred *from* conception—as you will learn in the next chapter. It can even be said that the soul knows the host *better* than the host knows him- or herself.

Remember, too, from Chapter Three that the soul returns to Heaven when its host dies. Since a sudden cardiac arrest *is* a death *if* the victim is *not* resuscitated, Cicoria's "ball of energy and thought" apparently was his soul *plus* something else that it carries to Heaven—and that the victim believes *is* the "real me."

The Real "Me"

Recall, too, Baptist minister Don Piper's joyful "visit to Heaven" in a previous chapter:

> "All of the people I encountered [in Heaven] were the same age they had been the last time I had seen them—except that all the ravages of living on earth had vanished [as had his too] … every feature was perfect, beautiful, and wonderful to gaze at. They embraced me, and no matter which direction I looked, I saw someone I had loved or who had loved me. They surrounded me, moving around so that everyone had a chance to welcome me to Heaven."

So Piper considered himself—and each of the others who welcomed him—as the "real him" and the "real them," respectively. This naturally meant that he was recalling soul memories of the *lifetimes* he had known of those individuals *and* himself.

Then, once Piper's body was resuscitated, his soul was "sucked back" into his body to continue the rest of his life on Earth, *almost* uninterrupted, except for his near-death experience and his reformed attitude about life on Earth.

Soul Past-Lives

Furthermore, during Brian Weiss' hypnotic regression of his patients, each of them "became" their soul's host in its specific *past* reincarnation in which that host had an emotionally traumatic experience, one which still plagued the patient in *this* life. Consider this example from Weiss' patient Catherine:

> "There are trees and a stone road. I see a fire with cooking. My hair is blonde. I'm wearing a long, coarse brown dress and sandals. I am twenty-five. I have a girl

child named Cleastra … There are big waves knocking down trees. There's no place to run. It's cold; the water is cold. I have to save my baby but I cannot … just have to hold her tight. I drown; the water chokes me. I can't breathe, can't swallow … salty waster. My baby is torn out of my arms."

Notice the apparent realism of Catherine's *reliving* the experience of that host in her soul's past life (i.e., past incarnation)—as the "real her," just as in Piper's case, the "real him." Obviously, however, that quotation was only a *snippet* of that host's *entire* lifetime.

Soul Immortal Memories

Now consider the following dialogue between Newton and his client with the very advanced soul, who was also mentioned in an earlier chapter:

N: "Why do spirits [i.e., souls] display two black glowing cavities for eyes when not showing a host's human form in the spirit world (i.e., Heaven)?
T: "The eyes you speak of represent a more concentrated intensity of thought. Rather than eyes, they are windows to old bodies [i.e., previous hosts] and all the physical extensions of former selves [i.e., previous hosts].''

Newton's question to his client with the very advanced soul was based upon *each* soul's unlimited creative ability. In Heaven, each may appear as one of its favorite hosts from its past incarnations. This client's hypnotically regressed answer (i.e., from her soul) suggests, however, that souls preserve immortal memories of *more* than just physical appearances of all their past hosts. Each immortal memory apparently includes that host's *whole life*—as was described in the first paragraph of this chapter and was illustrated in Catherine's testimony.

In support of this idea, Michael Newton writes the following in his book *Memories of the Afterlife*: "Scientists are learning that subatomic particles, acting under the influence of vibrational energy waves, both record and store all images, animate and inanimate, on Earth. Events represent patterns of pure vibrational energy so that no human experience is ever lost that cannot be recovered for analysis in the timeless afterlife."

Therefore this seems to substantiate why near-death survivors naturally consider his- or her whole-life soul memory "the real him" or "the real her."

Analysis of NDE "Separation" and "Sucking Back"

Whether a sudden cardiac arrest victim has a stage one (i.e., out-of-body) NDE as Cicoria did, or a stage two (i.e., "visiting Heaven") as Piper did, may depend upon the length of time and/or difficulty of resuscitation of the physical body, as the soul might follow its usual path to Heaven.

Of course, the soul typically goes to Heaven *only* at the death of its host. But the spirit world seems to providentially defy death for NDE survivors that "visit Heaven," as well as for *all* NDE survivors to be sucked back into their resuscitated bodies—and resume life almost uninterrupted, except for their sudden cardiac arrest, their near-death experience, and any possible attitude reform about life on Earth.

However, metaphysical studies and literature mention a "silver cord," also known as the "sutratma" or "life thread of the antahkarana," referring to a so-called "life-giving linkage" that is severed from the physical body *only* at mortal death. Regardless, there seems to be some connection with Heaven, as in the comment that many NDEers report receiving when they do "visit Heaven": "You must go back; your time is not yet!"

Therefore, it seems a reasonable presumption for this book to suggest that the sudden cardiac arrest victim's *immediate* deprivation of normal human faculties *induces* in him or her a "real me" a sensory state like Catherine's, described earlier—since the sudden cardiac arrest victim *is* his or her soul's *host* in its *present* incarnation. Both Catherine's and the victim's sensory states were in the absence of life and both were enabled by their soul's immortal whole-life memory.

The immortal *whole-life* soul memory seems correct in another way too. Some NDE survivors who "visit Heaven" have told of witnessing a life review. But it includes *only* that part of the victim's life *up to* his or her sudden cardiac arrest—as you would expect, wouldn't you?

Furthermore, in the soul's meetings with its Council of Elders, every aspect of its *host's* life seems transparent to Council members—as souls are said to be "transparent" to one another too.

Another means of support is the legendary Akashic Books of Life, in which souls can find immortal records of every deed, thought, and activity in *any* of their incarnations. These records have been described as involving everything that happened during the human's (i.e., host's) lifetime, including other people who were affected *from their point of view,* with life-like sensations. Soul groups study these dynamic "replays" in Heaven to learn alternative actions and outcomes, apparently in real time!

Therefore, it seems beyond human understanding how, when, and why near-death experiences vary in the manner that they do. However, it is known that souls exist, they are incorporeal, and, as Cicoria described, a "ball of energy." So this book must conclude that a *more definitive* explanation of near-death experiences seems far beyond science and religion, now and perhaps forever.

The next chapter discusses how souls were found in the womb.

Chapter Eleven

How Souls Were Discovered in the Womb

Remember, too, from an earlier chapter "memories of which you are *not* aware—that come from *other* forms of "consciousness" of which you also are *not* aware." One was discussed there; this chapter discusses the second kind.

Until recently, medicine still considered the time before birth to hold little importance. This may have seemed reasonable considering that the fetus remains "undisturbed" in medicine's historic view and fetal studies are recent developments.

Yet this chapter begins with an age-old question whether *threatened* abortion might later affect the mind and personality of the growing child. It leads to the subject of this chapter and a second kind of "hidden" memories—from the womb!

A Very Special Case

Toward the end of the last century, fascinating details began to emerge about fetal "memories." But "memories" from the womb certainly would *not* seem possible with fetuses' immature brains. Yet, as far back as 1979, Canadian psychotherapist Andrew Feldmar documented an unusual case. This involved four unrelated male teenage patients, who each had attempted suicide once a year at least five times. The time of year for each one's effort differed, yet for each the date remained about the same for *every attempt.* Suspecting some link, the therapist did probing interviews with each of the four mothers. Each admitted having secretly attempted abortion, ironically on about the same time of year that her son later attempted suicide.

So Feldmar suspected that those four teenagers apparently had somehow "sensed" that they were not worth living, but without realizing why. Yet eventual admissions by the mothers to their sons ended their sons' suicide efforts. So the psychotherapist concluded, "Once the [conscious] connection is made, the child is relieved of compulsively having to act out the [unconscious] memory." This confirmed uterine memory and learning while answering age-old questions about how *threatened* abortion might later affect the mind and personality of the growing child.

But obviously, a single case like this is *not* sufficient to form a scientific conclusion. So a joint European study followed the children of hundreds of parents for as long as *twenty-five years* after birth. This book cannot possibly report all of the *undesirable* traits and the socio-behavioral and learning *problems* manifested by the *rejected* kids throughout the study. But those *negative* outcomes were relatively *absent* in children whose parents welcomed them. That study was published as "Born Unwanted: Developmental Effects of Denied Abortion" by Avicenum: Prague, 1988.

Any reasonable person might have expected that *unwanted* children might manifest some such problems. But the odds contrasting the predominance of *unwanted* kids' problems to favorable outcomes for the *wanted* children seem overwhelming.

Yet, if any readers still feel that memories from the womb must involve the fetal brain—even an immature one—a 2008 Swedish/French research project by Lagercrantz and Changeux entitled their report "The Emergence of Human Consciousness: From Fetal to Neonatal Life." Results were published the next year in the peer-reviewed professional journal *Pediatric Research*. The abstract says, "The fetus may be aware of the body, for example by perceiving pain. It reacts to touch, smell, and sound, and shows facial expressions responding to external stimuli. However, these reactions are probably preprogrammed and have a subcortical nonconscious origin."

Neurology of Hypnosis

Although hypnotic regression was discussed in the previous chapter, neurological details of that procedure were withheld until now. As you will find, hypnotic regression is simply a facilitated method of deep relaxation, wherein the subject's focus of attention gradually shifts away from the typically "busy" awareness of daily cares. That makes it more acceptable to patients who might have been uneasy about exploring emotional trauma from childhood and later, and it became a traditional procedure for psychotherapy.

Yet, so-called "past-lives" and "life-between-lives" were inconceivable to psychologists and psychiatrists in the past. This therefore caused the discoverers of these two "states of mind" to be shocked and initially to disbelieve, as you read in the earlier chapter. In this chapter you will read that some other psychotherapists, while treating adult patients with *traditional* hypnotic regression, were confronted with virtually impossible patient memories *from within their mothers' wombs* (i.e., as fetuses).

The public's attitude toward hypnosis probably has been distorted by stage entertainment and people's common sense. Anyone watching a hypnotist perform has witnessed the power of suggestion. Less well understood is the meticulous care that medical hypnotherapists must take to "avoid leading the witness," so to speak. In order to keep from coaching their patients and thereby possibly inducing false memories, clinical psychotherapists bear a grave responsibility.

Despite such precautions, however, the public still seems to distrust the results of hypnotic regression. This is especially prevalent in reports of past-lives and life-between-lives. Yet, perhaps the public simply does not believe in any results of hypnosis.

Seeking the Source of Hidden Fetal Memories

Brian Weiss and Michael Newton *accidentally* discovered that we each have a God-given soul in our right hemisphere through hypnotic regression. But another psychotherapist—also using *traditional* hypnotic regression with adult patients for traumatic memories from their *early childhood*—was stymied by an assortment of spontaneous responses apparently *from the womb!*

California psychotherapist David Chamberlain released his earlier research experiences in his 1988 book *Babies Remember Birth: And Other Extraordinary Scientific Discoveries About the Mind and Personality of Your Newborn.* This happened primarily as the result of the many surprising yet *spontaneous* responses he heard from his *adult* patients in *traditional* hypnotherapy.

Chamberlain spoke about how this happened: "I didn't know that people could remember birth so I just said 'Go back to when you first felt this way' [i.e., emotional trauma]. And they would go places like [i.e., their] birth or into the [i.e., their mothers'] womb and this was a total revelation to me. What I realized was that there was something there [i.e., in the womb] before the brain. It took me a while to name it but there was human awareness, a human consciousness, a human intelligence that was not accounted for by brain development."

Chamberlain's intriguing online article "One Well-Hidden Secret of Good Parenting" paints the picture of "a [typical] prenate with at least a dozen senses, keen awareness of pain and danger, actively reaching out to communicate, and finding it difficult to cope with unloving events like neglect and silence."

In his 2013 book *Windows to the Womb: Revealing the Conscious Baby from Conception to Birth,* Chamberlain reveals, "While brain matter has no explanatory power for such memories or any other manifestations of intelligence, emotion, or purpose during this time period, the evidence for *consciousness* remains pervasive and continuous. Thus, with no brain matter to explain them, memories continue to form and consciousness supports the human memories found at conception, shortly after conception, and the significant stream of events well *before* conception. Even more impossible to explain are the memories 'babies' display about interactions and relationships that occur over an extended period from months to years before the conception itself."

Examples of these fetal traits include, but are not restricted to, the following:

• Aware of the mother's, father's, and sibling's attitude about the pregnancy or toward the fetus.
• Sense imminent danger for the mother or fetus, such as umbilical cord caught around the neck, and even warn the mother psychically.
• Realize any consideration of its being aborted.
• Traumatized emotionally by maternal environment, such as loud noises or fire.
• Hostile toward the birth mother for being given away for adoption.

Researcher Jenny Wade's exhaustive investigation of the existence of an independent anomalous "consciousness" in the womb with the fetus culminated in her *Birth Psychology* article "Two Voices from the Womb." The abstract reads:

"In recent years, prenatal research has demonstrated that fetuses are far more sophisticated than previously thought, findings generally ignored by the medical and psychological establishment in part because the neurological structures traditionally associated with mentation were not believed to be functional. Recent research on memory suggests that consciousness may not be dependent on the central nervous system, or even on the body. Using each major theory of memory and neurological research to examine the prenatal data, this paper concludes that two sources of consciousness are present before and during birth constructing a single subjective experience of self."

Prenatal and Perinatal Psychology

Now there is increasing acceptance of *experiential* evidence manifested by emotionally traumatic memories from the womb and surrounding birth. It must be emphasized, however, that prenatal (i.e., before birth) and perinatal (i.e., surrounding birth) psychology is not restricted to research *alone* but equally—or even more important—it is dedicated to reaching out to health care practitioners! But the extraordinary nature of those discoveries and the resulting psychotherapy is naturally so revolutionary that traditional professional attitudes and beliefs are hard to change.

Yet, prenatal and perinatal psychology is now recognized in the United States as the Association for Prenatal and Perinatal Psychology and Health (APPPAH). It has a growing membership and participation in both research and practice. It has published its own quarterly journal for twenty-eight years and hosted its Twenty-Second Annual International Congress in 2017. It also has an Italian companion organization. The APPPAH website is http://birthpsychology.com.

In his 2013 book, Chamberlain also writes, "Hypnotherapy, primal therapy, psychedelic therapies, various combinations of bodywork with breathing and sound stimulation, sand-tray therapy, and art work have all proved useful in accessing important imprints, decisions, and memories stored in the infant mind."

Incredible Unless Witnessed Personally

It is obvious that prenatal and perinatal psychology is nearly impossible to appreciate except from personal experience, so excerpts are offered from an interview with APPPAH-member Wendy Anne McCarty:

"Looking back, I was coming from a traditional western Newtonian paradigm way of understanding babies and the beginning of life. APPPAH didn't really fit with my previous education and training about babies and early development. Then, in 1988, I came to an APPPAH conference for the first time and literally my world was turned upside down.

"It was actually William [Emerson, PhD] showing a video from a therapy session with a young baby that gave me a direct experience of seeing the baby's deeper capacities and the mutual "communication" between them. That's when I had a profound "ah-ha" moment. William interacted with the baby from a whole different premise than I had ever seen, and with that more "conscious" interaction, I saw how the baby responded in ways I didn't know possible. When I watched the video with William as our guide, I experienced something with that baby that just changed everything for me."

Now there is increasing acceptance of *experiential* evidence manifested by emotionally traumatic memories from the womb and surrounding birth. Several quotes from literature in prenatal and perinatal psychology suggest that the *source* of such memories have advanced attributes. These include:

"Birth memories contain so much wisdom and caring, analytical thinking and perspective, and other manifestations of higher consciousness, they raise fundamental questions about the nature of persons.
"An innate mind, personal yearnings, spunk, spirit, and purpose. They can exhibit telepathy (i.e., thought communication), clairvoyance (i.e., seeing objects or events beyond the five senses), out-of-body perception, and transcendent awareness."

Parenthetically, however, it is very important to recognize the common problem that exists for psychotherapists seeking to address hidden memories—whether from the womb or from early years after birth. Since infants with hidden memories from the womb *seem to have* no means of expressing themselves, therapists like William Emerson (i.e., in Wendy McCarty's interview) must develop special empathic techniques for interacting with the infant. So consider, too, research pioneer Allan Schore's recommendations of a revolutionary approach for addressing "hidden" memories from early childhood, for use later in the patient's life.

Schore's words may help explain William Emerson's special technique:

"In the critical moments of any session the patient must sense that we (i.e., psychotherapists) are empathically with them. Research shows a difference between the left-brain understanding of cognitive empathy and right brain bodily-based emotional empathy. Intuition and empathy are right-brain functions, and both operate at levels beneath conscious awareness."

This appears in David Bullard's online interview of Allan Schore about Schore's 2012 book *The Science of the Art of Psychotherapy*.

From Other Researchers

Psychoanalyst Helen Wambach embarked upon research in the nineteen seventies to find answers beyond her private practice and teaching. In 1979, she released her first report in her book *Life Before Life*. This covered seven hundred and fifty *adult* subjects she had hypnotized into their mothers' wombs. The majority described their womb experiences as containing two "separate and simultaneous sources of awareness."

Those individuals described a "transcendent voice [that] tended to be devoid of emotion and characterize itself as a disembodied mind hovering around the fetus and mother, being in and out of the fetus. The other vantage point they reported was from the fetal human body, a perspective that was characteristically more visceral and filled with strong emotions."

Thousands of other patients hypnotically regressed into their mothers' wombs reported similar observations there. They too reported two distinct sensibilities—one was a wet, cramped somatic (i.e., body) feeling and the other was an advanced awareness, intelligence, or "consciousness" far beyond the capability of the immature fetal brain.

In APPPAH-member Wendy Anne McCarty's 2009 book *Welcoming Consciousness: Supporting Babies' Wholeness from the Beginning of Life* she expands on "fetal consciousness" with an unusual personal claim. She writes, "Underlying all of my [regression] experiences, I found I had a clear sense of myself. Often I was in the midst of a viscerally intense experience, yet I also had a *witness self* that was experiencing it from a much broader perspective. I never experienced an interruption of my sense of self." McCarty's Website is "Wondrous Beginnings" (http://www.wondrousbeginnings.com).

Soul Consciousness?

Researcher Jenny Wade's article "Physically Transcendent Awareness: A Comparison of the Phenomenology of Consciousness Before Birth and After Death" appeared in a 1998 issue of the *Journal of Near-Death Studies*. In it she acknowledged that our typical understanding of consciousness is *"a brain-based source of awareness which gives us our everyday experience of the world."* But she believes that *"consciousness"* also can provide *"a physically transcendent source of awareness"* which "predates physical life and survives bodily death." She calls this additional state the "transcendent source of consciousness" (TSC).

Wade emphasizes that TSC is "particularly likely to be prominent in prenatal and near-death experiences, as well as in mystical states of consciousness, but this tends to be damped out by brain-based consciousness [i.e., ego] during most of the [human] life span." She says that TSC "is pre-existent [to human life] and, as it were, 'attaches itself' in an individualized form [i.e., with the body] during the course of human life." Wade insists that human beings enter this world "wired with a dualistic spatiotemporal orientation" which enables them to "realize through spiritual practice or some other way" how to access their transcendent source of consciousness.

Wade does not use the term "soul" for her "transcendent source of consciousness." However, footnotes in her 1996 book *Changes of Mind* do acknowledge her reluctance to use the word "soul" because she feels that it is "not sufficiently academic."

The next chapter is a complete discussion of our God-given souls.

Chapter Twelve

Our God-Given Souls

Remember that Michael Newton reported that he found one hypnotically regressed woman's "span of [soul] incarnations staggering, going far back into the distant past of human life on Earth." Her (i.e., soul's) first lives (i.e., incarnations) occurred "at the beginning of the last warm interglacial period which lasted from 130,000 to 70,000 years ago, before the last great Ice Age spread over the planet."

This *fact* may *not* be comfortable to grasp—yet it is the *most* valid claim in human history, since our souls are immortal. God did *not* give any human being an option. Therefore, as you follow the specific details in this chapter, please remember that reincarnation *was* a part of Christian orthodoxy in Jesus' day.

Yet, it is obvious that the spiritual processes involved in reincarnation were *not* revealed to humankind until the recent advances described in the earlier chapters. So, as you read the spiritual details discussed here, we almost have to accept that these, too, were part of "God's Grand Plan."

With the dramatic expansion of Earth's population, God continues creating new souls as will be illustrated later in this chapter. Since souls start incarnating on Earth soon after they are created, however, some souls may be further advanced in spiritual growth than others that have not been reincarnating as long.

Souls have been called "sparks of God," perhaps because they are individually formed and imbued with seeds of His capabilities—that can be developed significantly in Heaven. Therefore, each soul's passion is to learn firsthand why and how human frailties exist even with, or perhaps because of, God gift of free will to every human. Yet, reincarnation allows all souls to grow in spiritual wisdom, with the possibility of melding their wisdom with more advanced souls in greater responsibilities in the Spirit World, and eventually in rejoining The Divinity.

But you and every other person reading this book must understand several other facts. First, no human being ever born on Earth was aware of his or her soul and its memories. Second, within the past three decades, only patients or clients who have been hypnotically regressed by their psychologist or psychiatrist have "met" their souls. Third, only when you die physically will the "real you" be part of your soul's immortal memory when it returns to Heaven.

So, as you read this chapter about souls, please keep in mind those two different—yet strangely similar—examples from an earlier chapter: Cicoria, a highly trained professional adult, described what separated from his body, leaving him as "just a ball of energy and thought" and Katie, the seven-year-old girl, who seemed to just float, unassuming but curious, throughout her home, before her parents were notified.

It seems that God gave us souls for three reasons. One was to express Its love as Its intermediary with each human being. Second was to enable souls to grow in spiritual wisdom, as they are able to help their hosts overcome human frailties. Third was to allow their hosts to have a spiritual counselor as an innate part of them, as an intimate source of help.

So this chapter will offer other details, many of which Michael Newton recorded from his hypnotically regressed patients and clients during his ten-year research hiatus from professional practice.

Creation of New Souls

Other comments from clients hypnotically regressed to their soul memories of Heaven (i.e., "life–between-lives") portray a limitless realm where thought is dominant and spiritual energy is the prime facilitator. One client's soul memory was as an Incubator Mother, working with the creation of new souls. Paraphrased from Newton's second book, the following was included:

> "The nursery is a vast emporium without outside dimensions. Under an archway, the entire wall is filled with a molten mass of high-intensity energy and vitality. It feels as if it is energized by an amazing love force. It pulsates and undulates in a beautiful flowing motion. From the mass, a swelling begins, never from the same site twice. The swelling increases and pushes out, becoming a formless bulge. It separates, with the birth of a new soul. We are in the delivery suite, where newly arrived ones are conveyed as small masses of white energy encased in a gold sac. Through us comes a life force of all-knowing love and knowledge. What we pass on with our vibrations is the essence of a beginning—a hopefulness of future accomplishment. This involves instilling thoughts of what they are and what they can become. When we enfold a new soul in a love hug, it infuses this being with our understanding and compassion. Each soul is unique in its totality of characteristics created by a perfection that I cannot begin to describe. I have a sense that there is a powerful Presence on the other side of the archway who is managing things. I feel that the Creator is ... close by ... but may not be doing the work of production ... I think there are others who assist—I don't know."

Your Soul

So while *your* soul was still in Heaven, for its next reincarnation it selected your human body, your family, and your life circumstances to join. That choice was made with the help of its spirit guide and Council of Elders, in regard to the soul's karmic balance and challenges it still must face in its reincarnations.

Your soul seemed to come first into your mother's womb, identified in the previous chapter as "fetal consciousness." Without your ever knowing it, once your soul united with your human fetus in your mother's womb it became an intimate part of your existence.

Documentation of soul testimonies, accessible through hypnotic client regression to their souls' "past-life" and "life-between-lives" trance states, has revealed the intimacy between soul and host. Those descriptions frequently are offered in the grammatical "first person," as if the soul is *actually* the host.

However, for humankind to realize that each person has a soul and to understand the implications that this holds for each of us and our loved ones, personal attention must rise above the present level of ignorance and disregard. It should not have to be necessary that each of us undergo a "near-death experience" to realize what the millions of near-death survivors learned.

Hemispheres

Then, when your brain's *left* hemisphere brought "waking" consciousness—but *not* until about age three—your ego began developing. Yet earlier, around the time of your birth, your *right* hemisphere was already operating. This continued until "waking" consciousness took over and became dominant in your life.

But your "right hemisphere" also had a "consciousness," like the one in your mother's womb. Obviously, your "waking" consciousness is alert *only* while you are awake—but your right hemisphere soul *never* sleeps! That is why your soul knows you better than you know yourself!

This is why it may be personally troubling to even consider whether we and our souls have conflicting beliefs, attitudes, goals, and the like. Differences may be insignificant unless they are extreme. Examples of dangerous contrasts have increasingly appeared on the world stage in roles of power hunger, greed, revenge, malevolence, and injustice.

But since your soul is subtle and non-controlling, it may have had stiff competition if you had a strong and dominating ego from your *left* hemisphere. Yet, even though you *never* were taught or knew this, your soul *unconsciously* influenced many of your thoughts, decisions, and actions.

In his article "The Quantum Physical Communication Between the Self and the Soul" published in the *Noetic Journal,* physicist Fred Alan Wolf wrote, "Communication between soul [self] and [body] self is difficult at best. Often the soul [self] is not heard or becomes devastated in its attempts to reach the deeply embodied and preoccupied [body] self … the language of the soul is not a language of logic and words, but instead is one that speaks through the heart and intuition, often most loudly when we are in deepest trouble."

But realize, too, that the individual soul in each of us has also had a past of its own. Its "past" consisted of being an incorporeal (i.e., non-material) part of many, many other families in its multiple reincarnations over perhaps many thousands of previous Earth lifetimes. Naturally, your soul's host in each past lifetime was a member of one of those families.

Naturally, persons who have had a spiritual (i.e., life-between-lives) regression "meet" their soul, so to speak, through its memories of Heaven after its previous incarnation on Earth—as will the rest of us after our physical death and our souls' return to Heaven. However, for readers interested in learning more about building a relationship with their souls while still here on Earth, a final chapter is included, "Messages From Our Souls."

Soul Details

Significantly, all souls are equal in God's eyes. No hierarchy exists among them. Each soul has a unique and immortal identity. This is like a "fingerprint," which Newton says relates to its formation, composition, and vibrational distribution. This helps establish their individuality and enables them to recognize one another. Souls in Heaven also have hues that identify their level of advancement and responsibility. There too, souls are neither male nor female in terms of human understanding, but may incarnate in a male or female body.

Souls innately possess an apparently unlimited and unexcelled consciousness with insight, conscience, imagination, honesty, intuition, intelligence, special senses beyond human comprehension, and creativity far beyond anything on Earth. Despite souls' *immaterial* (i.e., incorporeal) composition, their ability to manipulate energy forces seems unlimited as "spirits." Souls also seem able to acquire an even more sophisticated creative ability through specialized experience in the spirit world. Newton says that souls can create anything they wish.

Soul Creative Ability

Souls therefore can appear as anything, anytime—including one of their hosts from any of their previous reincarnations. For example, Newton's hypnotic regression clients describe how they, as souls, may appear in Heaven as one of their favorite past-life hosts, instead of their regular "spirit" appearance. Apparently, fellow souls expect this and may do so too. The following two incidents therefore are offered as apparently true, but without any possible explanation—unless they are manifestations of souls' capabilities from Heaven.

This first experience in the late Elizabeth Kubler-Ross' book on LIFE after DEATH is mind-blowing but her sincerity and integrity are unquestionable. It is from her 1977 speech "There Is No Death" in San Diego, California. She describes an unearthly experience that may illustrate the soul's unlimited creativity. Kubler-Ross had decided to quit her demanding work with death and dying patients. A woman approached her in the hall and asked to talk with her. But the psychiatrist had a strange feeling about the visitor. This person resembled a Mrs. Schwartz whom Kubler-Ross had known in her work, but that lady had died ten months earlier.

So, as they entered the office, the doctor touched the woman's skin, which seemed tangible enough. The visitor pleaded with Kubler-Ross not to forsake her work. Wisely, Kubler-Ross said, "You know Reverend Gaines is in Urbana now. He would just love to have a note from you. Would you mind?" She handed the woman a piece of paper and a pencil. After writing the note, the visitor frowned as if "Are you satisfied now?" as she handed it back to Kubler-Ross. When the woman stood up to leave, she repeated, "You promise?" Kubler-Ross' book reads, "And the moment I said, 'I promise,' she disappeared. We still have the note."

Not long ago the author recalled an event in his life that happened while he was still a young skeptic. Back then I simply discounted that experience with nothing more than great relief and gratitude. In light of Kubler-Ross' experience, I now wonder. At that time, my mother had been hospitalized twice and eventually was unable to care for herself. So I went to her apartment back in Virginia to see what could be done. Hopelessly mired in doubt and worry, I heard a knock on the apartment door. There stood a huge middle-aged woman with a small, scruffy suitcase in her hand. She said simply, "I'm here to care for your mother." Awestruck, I welcomed her in.

For the next year or so this woman took over all responsibilities for Mama. She slept on a futon, cashed Mama's Social Security checks, paid the rent and utility bills, and shopped, cleaned, and cooked for my mother. She had a rather gruff way about her, kept to herself, and wouldn't engage in conversation. She refused to be paid.

When Mama was taken to the hospital again and I was told she would need nursing home care, I rushed home to close the apartment, move her furniture out, and make necessary arrangements. The woman had disappeared without saying anything to anyone. To this day no one knows who she was, where she came from, or where she went. Nor did anyone ever speak of seeing her. I now consider her some sort of compassionate spiritual being. Yet I also believe that the woman might have been my beloved maternal grandmother who died almost 70 years ago—and was therefore also my mother's mother!

Imagine what that might mean about souls and Heaven—the energy of love is powerful enough to alert my grandmother's soul of my mother's problem—and mine caring for her—and create this woman to care for her!

Creation by Souls

The quotations appear in Michael Newton's first and second books, about his clients hypnotically regressed to their souls' "life-between-lives" memories. These creative skills begin with Level III souls and improve through Level V. He writes:

"Souls are expected to begin familiarizing themselves with the forces of creation by the time they are solidly established in Level III. The formation of inanimate to animate objects from the simple to the complex is a long slow process. With practice comes improvement but not until they approach Level V do my clients begin to feel they might actually contribute to the development of living things." (Remember that souls do not breath and do not require water or nutrition.)

The following are examples, from Level III through Level V souls:

"We can learn to create and see life developing on younger worlds with simpler organisms and without intelligent life.
"I'm not ready for living things yet. I experiment with the basic elements to create planetary substance ... rocks, air, and water ... keeping everything very small.
"I start with creating embryos.
"We have gathered for practice in creation training with our energy. Trinity is standing at a chalkboard drawing how to make a mouse quickly.
"We are to rapidly visualize a mouse in our minds ... as to the necessary energy parts to create a whole mouse. There is an order of progression with how energy should be arranged in any creation.
"A soul who becomes proficient with actually creating life must be able to split cells and give DNA instructions by sending particles of energy into protoplasm."

Reunions With Departed Loved Ones in Heaven

Naturally, that last example raises an unmentioned concern some readers may have, in addition to the author: "Will we be reunited with our previously departed loved ones in Heaven?" Newton said, "Souls also may appear as their previous human hosts when greeting near-death victims and souls 'returning home'." Remember Baptist minister Don Piper's words after his NDE "visiting Heaven": "Never, even in my happiest moments, had I ever felt so fully alive. I stood speechless in front of the crowd of loved ones."

Newton also claims that the soul can take only a *fraction* of its energy to a reincarnation. So a part of our soul always remains in Heaven, always available for reunions with our departed loved ones during an NDE "visit to Heaven" or when our soul eventually returns to Heaven.

Perhaps, you—like the author—might feel awed by the apparent mysteries of the spirit world.

Soul Variables

From the time of their creation, each soul somehow surmises that it is a minute spark from our Creator. This therefore encourages *most* of them to grow in spiritual wisdom through repeated incarnations on Earth.

The word "most" seems appropriate here because each so-called "soul self" has an individual set of traits like humans do. Examples include "courageous," "quiet," "adventurous," "tenacious," "passive," "aggressive," "serious," "fun loving," "domineering," "action oriented," and "cautious." Naturally, these factors are important in how compatible a soul's traits are with a newborn's temperament.

Moreover, souls may have weaknesses or strengths, just as developing humans can. So a stable match is desirable. Of course, a soul's motivation may vary too, especially after one or a series of difficult incarnations. Although souls are considered immortal and indestructible, an incarnation with an egregious host can contaminate the soul's energy. But restoration is possible in the spirit world.

Soul Groups and Activities

Souls begin in a "primary" group of about seven to twelve members, which enables them to know one another well and to develop close bonds that last forever. Remember Newton's patient who got so lonely, missing fellow members in her primary group? Primary groups also are composed of assorted traits for balance. Members of each primary group are basically at the same level of development. But a soul's strengths, potential for growth, and degree of motivation may qualify it for advancement. Any who develop faster therefore may be moved to more advanced groups.

Souls that may incarnate "together"—for example in different hosts, living at a similar Earth time, or perhaps "connected" as family or extended family members—also develop close relationships in the spirit world. Such affiliations form so-called "secondary groups" that may contain a thousand or more souls—but incarnating with one-another only intermittently.

During its existence at home in the spirit world, each soul therefore interacts with countless other souls. This enables many groups to become very close-knit and may involve so-called "soul mates." Souls will also meet with spirit guides, teachers, and counselors, as well as with their Council of Elders.

Souls can participate in a wide variety of activities, for further learning, recreation, and service. They also may have time alone for thought and development. Special energy "immersion" experiences are available to sharpen their sensitivity to other forms of life or to recharge soul energy.

The mention of pets demands an explanation: souls may also develop bonds with human family members and their pets. Also, the soul of a family member may be a soul mate for the host's soul.

Humans sometimes call the goal of our souls' spiritual growth "enlightenment." But achievement of enlightenment should never be viewed with any feeling of self-righteousness, as might be typical of the human ego. Rather, spiritual advancement is viewed by the soul with great humility, as is expressed in these lines from an ancient poem by a Chinese Zen master: "Before enlightenment, chop wood, carry water; after enlightenment, chop wood, carry water."

All Work and No Play?

Michael Newton's book *Destiny of Souls* contains a section entitled "Leisure Time," acknowledging that the afterlife (i.e., Heaven) also offers leisure time, including recess breaks from learning, occasional quiet solitude, recreational or educational trips, and visits with beloved deceased pets, as well as dancing, music, and games that foster camaraderie among residents.

Soul Relationships

Regardless of a soul's stage of development, each one treats all other souls with humility, respect, conviviality, and dignity. Souls are said to value honesty with themselves and with other souls as a prime virtue. They seek and welcome feedback from other souls as a means of spiritual growth. They willingly offer feedback to other souls, completely devoid of judgment. That growth is central to each soul's advancement.

In the spirit world, advanced souls may have an enhanced ability and opportunity to demonstrate compassion, love, caring, and empathy. Therefore, they may be recognized and respected for those talents in counseling and helping less advanced souls. The unconditional love demonstrated by souls for one another is unparalleled on earth. It is best considered to be a reflection of the unconditional love and empathy exemplified by our Creator.

Soul Advancement

The opportunities for growth, specialization, and service in Heaven are viewed by souls with great humility. Newton's examples include Nursery Teachers, Harmonizers, Masters of Design, Explorers, and Archivists. Such very advanced souls therefore may not need to reincarnate.

Furthermore, the number of reincarnations that a soul may have had could reach thousands or more. If this number seems incredible, please realize that, generally speaking, souls' advancement in spiritual wisdom is individual. This also reflects their immortality. Plus, there is no competition in Heaven.

Soul Self-Accountability

God gives each of us a unique soul. So our soul therefore feels responsible to fulfill the three-fold intent of each incarnation: to learn; to develop spiritually; and to help its host. Yet, only by being a part of the circumstances that confront humans, can souls learn why and how we act and react as we do. Naturally, our souls *usually* can view this with a much broader perspective than we humans can. This thereby may help both the soul and its host to avoid human frailties, like jealousy, hate, and vengeance.

Souls' "self-accountability" is so foreign to most humans that it deserves an explanation. By contrast, some of us seem to pride ourselves on how much dishonesty we can "get away with," apparently justifying it to ourselves—and to others if we are caught—as "being deserved." Yet it may be *no* surprise that souls *willingly* manifest self-accountability—accepting *karmic* debts charged for *their hosts'* selfish acts, as well as karmic credits for his or her acts of compassion, for example.

Soul self-accountability offers a different way to view the earthly concept of so-called "judgment," especially as the latter is often perceived *incorrectly* as God's role to judge and punish human behavior.

Yet, think back to how God's punishment was portrayed in art, literature, and drama—bodies tortured relentlessly in hell. But you now should be able to realize that our physical bodies do *not* survive mortal death. Dead bodies are cremated or disintegrate in the grave! Moreover, since human bodies do *not* survive, anyone who expects special *human* privileges in Heaven as a terrorist *martyr* will be sadly disappointed. Naturally, this fact will *not* be realized until perhaps it is too late to change!

Guardian Angels?

Many people claim to have guardian angels and questions have been raised by life-threatening events where victims were mysteriously rescued. Newton says that his clients or patients in hypnotic regression never speak of these guardian spirits, but perhaps they are other unknown spirit entities.

Spirit Guides

Having the body "self" accept the soul "self" as a partner can be difficult, especially for a young or immature soul. Apparently, however, "young" souls are not left alone and may need help from "soul" or "spirit" guides in adjusting to their human hosts. But all immature souls are not "young." Rather, immaturity is a stage of the soul's spiritual growth over multiple incarnations on earth. "Young" souls may have had only one or two incarnations.

Guides can best be understood as spiritual teachers or counselors, serving needed roles for our souls. Soul guides usually are advanced souls who have incarnated and been selected for their special qualifications. Any souls working as guides, apart from the senior one, are often in guide training.

Veil of Forgetfulness

Acknowledging soul self-accountability could seem to be more humanly demanding, since our souls are immortal, yet they are part of us that we likely deny because of the legendary "veil of forgetfulness." The Christian New Testament quotation most often quoted in Satterfield's online references is from the Apostle Paul's first letter to the Corinthians 13:12:

"For now we see through a glass, darkly; but then face to face: now I know in part; but then shall I know even as also I am known."

This appears to contrast human consciousness before, and soul consciousness after, death of the mortal body. It therefore seems quite possible that our souls hold the answer to two haunting questions: "Why am I here?" and "Is this all there is to life?"

Realizing the reality of our souls should help persuade each of us that we are much more than our body, our personality, our achievements, our possessions—and, likewise—than our wealth, power, and privilege. We all are eternally connected through our souls.

But the "veil" keeps us from being *consciously* aware of our soul and soul memories, so we cannot use lessons that our souls learned previously during our present lives. This makes every incarnation a new challenge for them. Souls accept the veil as a condition for reincarnation.

Power of Thought

The afterlife is described as a place of pure thought. Moreover, "thought energy"—a capability unknown to us—seems to be the basis for many soul activities. Communication, creative skills, and even travel seem orchestrated by "thought." (Remember Katie's "travels"?). Souls can "see," reason, learn, create, and move freely. Michael Newton says that an outstanding characteristic of the spirit world is "a continuous feeling of a powerful mental force facilitating everything in uncanny harmony." His patients and clients call the spirit world "a place of pure thought."

Except in special situations where souls are encouraged to "block" their thoughts, telepathy makes each soul's thoughts transparent to other souls. This obviously prevents human practices of deceit, hidden agendas, and ego defenses. But blocking is imposed after a soul's meeting with its Council of Elders, to keep the proceedings secret from other souls and thus prevent second-guessing.

The next chapter discusses Creation and the Divinity

Chapter Thirteen

Creation and the Divinity

You probably have noticed that nothing so far in this book has described the Divinity—the One we call God or Allah. Yet, even very advanced souls apparently don't have access to God or even to knowledge about the Eternal Almighty. But all souls seem to feel that they are inherently part of the One they call the "Source." As such, souls look forward to being considered worthy enough to eventually join the "Old Ones"—in higher levels of responsibility—and eventually in conjunction with the Source.

Even the concept of time as we know it seems different in that which we call "Heaven" or the "spirit world." Perhaps because it is eternal, everything is "now"—there are no "yesterday" or "tomorrow." Apparently, however, this does not mean what we would call "simultaneous," despite human terminology of "past soul lives" (i.e. past incarnations).

Nevertheless, Michael Newton's second book *Destiny of Souls* does contain almost two-dozen references to what is termed "The Presence." This is powerfully felt in souls' meetings with their Council of Elders. The Presence has been described as a "pulsating purple or violet light," perceptible to all spirit entities that attend such meetings. It apparently emanates from above (i.e., overhead of) the proceedings. When describing council meetings, subjects in a life-between-lives trance comment that their souls cannot focus on this light because it would distract them from discussions with council members.

The Presence is considered a "higher force," not necessarily singular or plural nor male or female. It apparently is representative of collective energy of infinite and eternal wisdom. Hypnotically regressed clients say that council members are the highest "power" (i.e., wisest ones) they encounter. But even council members don't seem to consider the Presence as the ultimate Divinity in the spirit world. No life-between-lives regressed subject has ever claimed to perceive or sense anything like "absolute perfection."

Yet, from all that you have read so far, you might understand why the author prefers the term "Eternal Almighty" to other terms of reverence. The Prophet Mohammed said that the Angel Gabriel brought him messages from Allah, recorded in the Quran. Other prophets apparently chronicled the Hebrew Old Testament. But although both texts mention souls, remember that only recently have souls' memories of past reincarnations and their stays in Heaven been accessible through hypnotic regression.

Yet remember that, in the past, all of humanity had to depend upon their prophets and interpretations of religious scriptures for the nature of God and Heaven, as was suggested in the section "Do We Really Know God or Allah" in Chapter Four. But now, through the opportunity of personal spiritual hypnotic regression, anyone can learn much more about both firsthand.

Thousands of documented case studies from patient and client hypnotic regression have revealed information never before available. Remarkably, soul memories of Heaven often refer to what they call the "Source." Yet, souls feel that Council members are the most spiritually "advanced" entities they encounter.

The word "advanced" is used to avoid any suggestion of hierarchy. As mentioned elsewhere, all souls have equal value in God's eyes. However, the terms "Wise Ones" and "Old Ones" are mentioned, too, in regard to achievement. The ultimate goal of every soul is to be considered eligible for eventual conjunction with the Source—from which they believe they were created. It therefore seems that these two additional levels of achievement might imply closeness to conjunction.

Also, near-death survivors who visited Heaven have returned with dramatically reformed feelings about God, Heaven, and life and death on Earth.

Creation of Life and Everything Humanly Perceptible

This is perhaps the most questioned and debated topic over the centuries since the Hebrew Old Testament Book of Genesis became known.

Then, about one hundred and fifty years ago an English naturalist named Charles Darwin published a treatise based on changes in life forms that resulted from characteristics in organisms and their environment, a process called "evolution." This theory lent itself to a scientific hypothesis that life on earth originated from natural forces and did not require action by God.

Remember this from Chapter Four:

> After creating everything that is, the Eternal Almighty must have also seen fit to allow species of life on Earth to modify their and their offspring's ability to survive and procreate on Earth by adapting to their changing environments. (This happens over multiple generations as DNA becomes modified for survival, then passed.)

More recently, a young University of Illinois graduate student named Stanley Miller published the results of an experiment in which he showed that amino acids could be produced in a spark chamber. Since amino acids are the precursors to proteins, this led scientists to believe that the creation of life itself was within their grasp. Although scientists continue trying to produce life in a test tube, no one has succeeded.

DNA

DNA has been an essential part of life forms from the dawn of creation. The DNA evidence suggests that these basic mechanisms controlling biological form became established before or during the evolution of multicellular organisms and have been conserved with little modification ever since. Adding to science's dilemma for producing test tube life therefore was the question of how these first genes developed.

It seems conceivable that the information provided in DNA was part of the creation of life forms. Werner Gitt's seminal book *In the Beginning was Information: A Scientist Explains the Incredible Design in Nature* stresses that there is "a unique coding system ... of biological information ... in each genome." Further, Gitt quotes the conclusion of the seventh International Conference on the Origins of Life held in Mainz, Germany: "There is no known law of nature, no known process, and no known sequence of events which can cause information to originate by itself in nature."

Several characteristics about this biological information illustrate Gitt's claim "The coding system used for living beings is optimal from an engineering standpoint." First, it can be described as three different forms: "constructional/creative, operational, and communication." Also, the information can be distinguished as "copied, reproduced, or creative." Qualitatively, the information ranges from "extremely important" to "trivial" or "harmful." Quantitatively, it varies according to "semantic quality, relevance, timeliness, accessibility, existence, and comprehensibility. This strengthens the argument that it was a case of purposeful design rather that a [lucky] chance."

In case DNA's small size might appear insignificant as a major barrier to the creation of life by scientists, some details about DNA may help us realize the enormity of intelligence incorporated in DNA. Scientists found that DNA contains an exquisite "language" composed of some three billion genetic letters. Lee Strobel's book *The Case for a Creator* contains a statement by Stephen Meyer, director of the Center for Science and Culture at the Discovery Institute in Seattle, WA "One of the most extraordinary discoveries of the twentieth century was that DNA actually stores information—the detailed instructions for assembling proteins—in the form of a four-character digital code." Meyer elaborated on this in his book *Signature in the Cell: DNA and the Evidence for Intelligent Design*.

It is hard to fathom, but the amount of information in human DNA is roughly equivalent to twelve sets of the *Encyclopedia Britannica*—an incredible three hundred and eighty-four volumes' worth of detailed information that would fill forty-eight feet of library shelves! Molecular biologist Michael Denton's book *Evolution: A Theory in Crisis* said "In their actual size—which is only two millionths of a millimeter thick—a teaspoon of DNA could contain all the information needed to build the proteins for all the species of organisms that have ever lived on the earth, and there would still be enough room left for all the information in every book ever written."

In Michael Newton's most recent book *Memories of the Afterlife: Life Between Lives Stories of Personal Transformation* he wrote, "I believe the forces of intelligent creation go far beyond the religious concept of an anthropomorphic god (i.e., having a human form or human attributes.) These spiritual forces ... indicate that creation of intelligent energy is so vast in our universe as to be incomprehensible to the human mind."

Even if science ever solves the dilemma of how DNA originated in life forms on earth, there remains the inevitable and inexplicable question: where did all this information come from?

The next chapter addresses reincarnation in more detail.

Chapter Fourteen

Reincarnation

Many of you may feel that souls are unfairly blamed for their hosts' thoughts and actions. Of course, our lack of awareness of our souls *does* leave us free to pursue personal self-gratification at the expense of others. True, some of us have temperaments that blend with our souls to produce personalities that allow us to manifest empathy, compassion, and benevolence. But there are just as many or more of us who, for whatever reasons, live without regard to the consequences of our thoughts and actions.

Implications of Reincarnation

Theologian Christopher Bache, professor of religious studies at Youngstown State University, suggested that reincarnation has provided a vital missing link in Western theology: "Theologians have never satisfactorily explained the purpose of suffering in a universe created by a loving God, nor why it is so inequitably distributed." But remember Mattie Stepanek, whose soul may have sacrificially chosen his brief life to help others grow spiritually? In his book *Lifecycles: Reincarnation and the Web of Life*, Bache also wrote, "It's ironic, really. Christianity has taught us that God, the name given the Ultimate Reality in life, is loving, benevolent, and completely trustworthy. Yet it has also taken from us the key we need to recognize this love."

Some theologians seem to feel that reincarnation may cause those who believe in it to feel able to dispense with the institutional aspects of the Christian Way. But remember that this was a common belief during Jesus' time. My own belief now is that the entire concept of soul, spirit world, and reincarnation stresses the importance of love in our relationships with one another, and that our lives are inexorably intertwined. The church provides the gathering place where we can learn and practice these important principles and reach out to others who need our help. If religious institutions embraced the existence of souls too, they could offer invaluable guidance in spiritual practice wherein their members could help rather than hinder their souls' development.

This chapter therefore describes the process that every soul uses in Heaven to reincarnate on Earth and join a human body. This requires that the soul first spend adequate time contemplating its objectives for its new life. Soul specialists naturally are involved, as are other souls that might incarnate with the soul, as you will soon learn

Quotations from Michael Newton's subjects hypnotically regressed to their souls' memories of the "life-between lives" (i.e., Heaven) are consistent among some seven thousand clients. So testimonies in his books involving these findings are simply representative, not unique. Therefore, before a soul reincarnates, as your and my souls did, each develops a plan—sometimes called a "pre-birth blueprint"—for the body it will join on Earth

Newton says, "Without knowing why, many people believe their life has a plan. Of course, they are *right*. Although amnesia (i.e., Veil of Forgetfulness) does prevent humans from having full conscious knowledge of this plan, the unconscious mind holds the key to spiritual memories of a general blueprint of each life."

Life Selection

"The vehicle of life selection provides a kind of time machine for souls, where they see some alternative routes to the main road. Although these paths are not fully exposed to our souls, they carry some of the road map to Earth." In *Journey of Souls*, Michael Newton expands on this as follows.

"In the place of life selection, our souls preview the life span of more than one human being within the same life cycle. When listening to my subjects describe all the preparations that go into picking a new physical body, I am constantly reminded of the fluidity of spiritual time. The soul-mind is far from infallible as it works in conjunction with a biological brain. Regardless of our soul level [of spiritual growth], being human means we will all make mistakes and have the necessity of engaging in midcourse corrections during our [reincarnated] lives. This will be true with any body we [i.e., our souls] select."

Ring of Destiny

As Newton said, the so-called "Ring of Destiny" enables souls to visually review a limited number of "bodies" for their incarnation, depending on a soul's goals for the new lifetime. For example, one soul wanted to join a body that could become a musician. It was offered bodies in New York City, Paris, Los Angeles, and Oslo. It chose New York City because it lived there in its short past life. When the approximate time frame and geographic location is decided and the body/life choice is made, each soul will make its selection.

Group Reincarnation

When planning a reincarnation from Heaven, a soul often meets with its "soul family" (i.e., a group of other souls with whom it has reincarnated in the past as Earth family members). It may also meet with other soul "friends" (i.e., other souls that it reincarnated with in the past) and with spiritual guides. Soul incarnation plans therefore are seldom completed *without* other souls being involved and often reincarnating as a group.

Souls that reincarnate "together"—for example in different hosts, living at a similar Earth time, and perhaps "connected" as family or extended family members—develop close relationships in Heaven. More was provided in an earlier chapter about soul relationships with one another, and different kinds of groups that develop in Heaven.

Readers also may be curious if, and how, group reincarnation might apply to them. Hypnotically regressed patients and clients experiencing their souls' past lives have made several remarkable observations. Often their remarks are about the souls of their *present* relatives or friends on Earth.

Recognition Class

Yet, there is another kind of recognition for which souls are trained *before* reincarnation. Newton covers this in the chapter "Preparation for Embarkation" just before the chapter "Rebirth" in his first book. He writes that souls do *not* go immediately to Earth after the preceding steps were taken "before a significant element of preparation occurs."

This follows up "Group Reincarnation" to assure that, to paraphrase Newton's clients in regression, "We will know what to look for in our next life. The 'signs' are placed in our minds now to jog our memories as humans. [Remember, of course, that after early childhood, the Veil of Forgetfulness deprives human consciousness of soul memories of past lives and Heaven—including these plans.] These are 'flags'—markers on the road of life." In Newton's paraphrased words, "Not only sort out the best choice of who the 'main player' is going to be in the next life, but coordinate this decision with the other players in this upcoming drama. Their parts can be altered by him or her and his or her part can be altered by any of them, because free will script changes can be made by any one of the characters while life is in progress."

Limited Lives

In instances of death of an infant or a fetus not carried to term—but not intentionally aborted—it has been shown that the soul will return in a future child, of the same or closely related parents.

A soul may select a life that will be short-lived, one that will be "special needs," or one that is physically limited, as examples. This is done to help balance its past karma, provide extra "credits" in its spiritual growth, or even help strengthen another person's spirituality.

Mattie Stepanek was a good example. He died at fourteen from a rare disease, after a full life helping people acquire empathy. He was frequently seen on The Oprah Show in his wheelchair and attached to tubes that kept him alive, talkative, and upbeat. His mother, Jeni, said that, from a very early age, Mattie felt that "his purpose for being on earth was to be a messenger, to make people smile despite challenges." She has the adult-onset kind and also lost three other children with the genetic disease, who died at earlier ages.

Your Soul's Arrival

Researchers first "detected" (e.g., Chamberlain) your soul in your mother's womb, identified in an earlier chapter as "fetal consciousness." Soon, without your ever knowing it, your soul united with your human fetus in your mother's womb. It became an intimate part of your existence.

Yet, your soul was very careful *not* to be considered an intruder. Since it is incorporeal rather than material flesh, it took up no additional space in your body. It also tried to blend with your natural temperament. So, by the time you were born, your "fetal consciousness" or soul "merged" *psychically* with your developing human *mind*, so you and it together could manifest a single personality. Does the Fetus Understand?

One soul's incarnation into the mother's womb involved this pertinent dialogue between Newton and the regressed subject:

Dr. N: "When the baby is born, does it have any conscious thoughts of who its soul is and the reasons for the attachment?"
S: (pause) "The child mind is so undeveloped it does not reason out this information. It does have parts of this knowledge as a means of comfort, which then fades. By the time I speak, this information is locked deep inside me and that's the way it's supposed to be."

So recall studies by Ian Stevenson in an earlier chapter, verifying that some young children *do* recall "their" previous physical lives, and sometimes even "their" deaths.

Consciousness

While you still were very young, a part of your brain (i.e., *left* hemisphere) brought "waking" consciousness. But this was *not* until about three years of age. Yet your *right* hemisphere was operating *when* you were born. This was especially intended to help prepare you for this world as a newborn.

Moreover, your *right* hemisphere *also* has a "consciousness," like the one in your mother's womb. Remember that your soul's memories of its past lives and of Heaven *are accessed* through hypnotic regression of *this* hemisphere! Recall, too, Allan Schore's words from the earlier chapter, about the *lifetime* significance of your right hemisphere as "the unconscious."

Immortality

Reincarnation is a commitment for immortality—our souls experience earthly lessons that will help their spiritual growth. Also, remember that souls who achieve spiritual wisdom through multiple reincarnations may be given greater responsibility in the spirit world. Yet, training and participating in the Olympics is not easy either. Still, from the soul's point of view, the challenge and the achievement from reincarnation can be just as great as becoming an Olympic Gold Medalist.

Apparently there are many opportunities for learning in the spirit world. But many souls realize that Earth is the most challenging place for mastering human frailties. Also, some souls relish the pleasures that only Earth can offer.

Memories From the Past

A remarkable account of reincarnations of Jews who died in the Holocaust was provided in Rabbi Yonassan Gershom's first book, *Beyond the Ashes: Cases of Reincarnation from the Holocaust* (1992). His second book, *From Ashes to Healing: Mystical Encounters with the Holocaust* (1996), provided firsthand accounts from fourteen people who suffered traumatic memories of the Holocaust. He stressed the idea that souls usually reincarnate within the culture they inhabited in prior lifetimes, but some of these stories are from Gentiles who may have had Jewish ancestors. Rabbi Gershom reinforced the idea that reincarnation teachings were preserved and still are being taught by the ultraorthodox Hasidim.

As mentioned earlier, University of Virginia professor of psychiatry Ian Stevenson devoted over forty years to carefully investigating and documenting more than two thousand cases of very young children who spontaneously remembered past lives. His 2000 book *Children Who Remember Previous Lives: A Question of Reincarnation* is a compelling report on his detailed analyses.

Some of Stevenson's young subjects spoke of being fathers or husbands and gave names of their children or wives. They also described where they had lived. Surprisingly, when the professor interviewed those identified in their homes, their names and the characteristics of the homes matched what the children had said. If the child accompanied the researcher, the child often recognized family members and called them by name.

Xenoglossy

One of the puzzling aspects of reincarnation is what is known as "xenoglossy." This is an apparent ability to speak fluently one or more foreign languages without having been exposed to them in this lifetime.

Stevenson devoted two books to xenoglossy. In one book, *Unlearned Language: New Studies in Xenoglossy,* he described the case of a thirty-seven-year-old woman who, under hypnosis, reverted to the speech and manner of a male. She spoke fluent Spanish, although she could not do so in a normal state of consciousness. Stevenson studied this woman for eight years and was unable to find an explanation through his usually meticulous investigative techniques.

In her book *Reincarnation: The Phoenix Fire Mystery*, Sylvia Cranston described the case of twin baby boys, children of the prominent New York physician Marshall W. McDuffie and his wife, Wilhelmina. The twins were heard talking to one another in a language that neither parent recognized. When the boys continued to do so, they were taken to the foreign language department of Columbia University, but no one there could identify it. A professor of ancient languages happened to hear them and identified it as Aramaic, a tongue spoken at the time of Jesus.

Other researchers in past life hypnotic regression have even reported that, when the subjects told of past lives in different cultures, they sometimes were able to speak in the language that was native to the particular culture at that time.

Child Prodigies

Another equally puzzling aspect of reincarnation is child prodigy. Child prodigies have shown amazing abilities in mathematics, music, and other fields. In one of his many books, *How to Know God,* Deepak Chopra suggested that anyone acquainted with geniuses and prodigies usually consider them exceptional. They seem to be reincarnations of notables from the past who had great intellect or talent.

Scott Pelley interviewed such a young musical prodigy on CBS's 60 Minutes on November 28, 2006. At twelve, the young man, Jay Greenberg, had already written five full-length symphonies. Sam Zyman, who taught Jay music theory at Juilliard School in New York City, had taught there for eighteen years. He said that Jay "is a prodigy of the level of the greatest prodigies in history … the likes of Mozart, Mendelssohn, and Saint-Sans." Jay said the compositions just appear in his head and he writes them down, even though he may not be able to play them. He wrote "The Storm," commissioned by the New Haven Symphony in Connecticut, in just a few hours.

Child prodigies have occurred throughout history and elicited awe and speculation. Doctors Lehndorff and Falkenstein told about a young boy from Lubeck, Denmark named Christian Henrich Heineken. In 1723, at two years of age, he had already become fluent in French and Latin. By three, he had written a history of Denmark, and by four, he had become a brilliant mathematician. He died of natural causes half a year later. This appeared in the 1955 *Archives of Pediatrics.*

Implications of Reincarnation

Theologian Christopher Bache, professor of religious studies at Youngstown State University, suggested that reincarnation has provided a vital missing link in Western theology:

"Theologians have never satisfactorily explained the purpose of suffering in a universe created by a loving God, nor why it is so inequitably distributed."

The church provides the gathering place where we can learn and practice these important principles and reach out to others who need our help. If religious institutions embraced the existence of souls too, they could offer invaluable guidance in spiritual practice wherein their members could help rather than hinder their own souls' development.

Remember the major implication of reincarnation is the difference in perspective between the soul and its host. A human host naturally is concerned about its life on Earth. But its soul is involved in many different lifetimes on Earth, each one with a new host.

The next chapter is devoted to the Eastern time-honored concept of karma.

Chapter Fifteen

Karma

Reincarnation therefore is accompanied by a concept called "karma." It holds an established position in Hinduism and Buddhism as "the ethical consequences of one's actions." Karma has differing meanings, especially between Eastern traditions and Western interpretations. In the Buddhist and Hindu sense, karmic actions will bear fruit at some future time, implicitly for the person or his or her family or descendents. Yet karma is used predominantly in a *negative* sense in the West. In this country, for example, the slang version of the term "karma" is often used on texting, on Facebook, and otherwise on the Internet. There, it typically means retribution, such as "*bad* karma" or "payback."

But in the spiritual sense, *our* words, thoughts, and actions—*negative* or *positive* in how *we* treat *others*—are charged against *or* credited *to our soul*. But it is willingly self-accountable for any karma it acquires.

Realize, however, that your soul has *no* control over its host's actions—only *you* do. Therefore, the lives of your soul's *future* hosts may be determined to help balance out *negative* karma from the lives of its *previous* hosts, including you. Have you ever heard the idiom, "Whatever goes around comes around?"

The term "karma" has been applied to the overall concept, to specific circumstances, and to individual behavior. Basically, it apparently involves debits or credits, like a bank account, that the soul accumulates over various incarnations.

Karma in the spiritual interpretation may seem harsh since our souls are held responsible for their hosts' behavior in each incarnation. But our lack of awareness or disavowal of our souls apparently makes no difference to karma. Souls seem to incarnate for the lessons they can learn about human nature—why and how human frailties occur. Each and every frailty involves how we treat others: jealousy, vengeance, retribution, envy, lust, and fraud—just to name a few.

Debates may still occur about free will. Some opponents believe in determinism—that our lives are divinely planned for us. The flaw in that reasoning is that the future for any one of us human beings can be changed at any time by ourselves *or* by someone else's *change of plans*. In a sense, we all are interdependent—someone you never met and don't know *now* can change your future, even from across the globe. Certainly, the spirit world may know the future for any one of us, but that future is a set of *alternatives* that depend on our and others' actions *today*.

In his book *Destiny of Souls*, Michael Newton offers this observation:

"Although karma is associated with justice, its essence is not punitive but one of bringing balance to the sum of our deeds in all past lives."

We naturally are unable to know the spirit world's actual assessment of souls' efforts and progress. However, it seems reasonable that council members would consider certain facts about each soul and its host. Any or all of the following could seemingly influence the host's attitude toward and treatment of others *and* the soul's success or lack of it in influencing its host:

• Soul's maturity.
• Soul's level of spiritual growth.
• Soul's mesh with host's temperament.

- Soul's weaknesses and strengths.
- Soul's personality.
- Host's implicit memories that threaten personal relationships.
- Host's organic or genetic brain defects.
- Host's extent of nurturance and self-esteem.
- Host's social and emotional maturity.
- Intensity of host's instinct and ego drives.

Edgar Cayce, the "sleeping prophet," claimed that thoughts, rather than actions or failures, trigger karma. This may be doubted. But it does appear that *thought energy* is a currency of the cosmos, as supposedly is recorded in the Akashic field (i.e., spiritual Books of Life).

For example, consider that the "shared-death experience" for a family to participate in their loved one's passing may be accompanied by a panoramic "life review" of memories from the life just lived. What better way to accept this than as a thought-energy based sort of "video replay"? Such "energy" seems far different from the ones known by science. But it may relate to the nature of souls and to medical cases known as "healing touch."

As this book acknowledges, we not only are *unaware* of our souls but we also typically pursue instinct and ego drives that serve our perceived "best interests." Only by honestly considering that we *might* have a soul and that this *might* have some worthwhile meaning for our loved ones and for us will anyone give this book much further thought.

The next chapter discusses unusual experiences that accompany the end of life.

Chapter Sixteen

End-of-Life Experiences

Dying and death are being studied today with unusual interest. Even though both are still dreaded by most people, researchers are finding that the end of life is not instantaneous—and death is not simple. Perhaps the primary reason dying and death may seem more complex in this book is its acknowledgment of our souls. Scientists and health professionals may still be criticized by their peers for linking the end of life with the spiritual. However, some prominent researchers are helping to bridge the chasm. This chapter therefore discusses dying and death from the perspective of a few of those researchers, using the new acronym "end-of-life" (EOL).

For example, emergency care and cardiopulmonary resuscitation specialist Sam Parnia's book *Erasing Death: The Science That is Rewriting the Boundaries Between Life and Death* stresses his special interest in near-death survivors' testimonies. The soul's departure from the mortal body is sometimes unevenly timed, sometimes lingering in comatose patients. Much research has been done on these experiences.

End-of-Life Research

Dying persons seem aware when death is approaching. Their comments and behavior typically are characteristic of what are now called "end-of-life" (EOL) experiences. British psychiatrist Peter Fenwick is internationally recognized for his "end-of-life" research.

One unusual kind of phenomena seems to attest to psychic actuality, when a dying patient claims to have been "visited" by a deceased loved one—but that "visitor" actually had died recently *without the patient's knowledge.* Deceased "visitors" apparently offer to return closer to the time of death and even to come and escort the patient to Heaven.

It has been reported that dying ones also seem able to time their departure. This might involve delay if the patient has an *unsettled* personal or business matter. It also might be the patient's choice to leave this earth while family members are absent. This seems in keeping with critical care physician Sam Parnia's claim that death is *not* an instant event.

Certain rare events also have occurred—strange animal behavior or clocks stopping—at the time of death. Remarkably, a particular cat in a northeastern medical facility became a media celebrity when staff nurses noticed that it would snuggle next to patients who soon died.

Much of British psychiatrist Peter Fenwick's life has been devoted to studying deathbed phenomena and what these mean in the greater picture of whether human beings are simply corporeal (i.e., material) creatures as science insists. His work seems to focus on soul consciousness and the soul's survival of mortal death. He has written several books, including *The Art of Dying, The Truth in the Light,* and *The Hidden Door.* Fenwick has developed a number of observations about dying, which he shared in a 2012 interview, "Dr. Peter Fenwick Discusses Dying, Death, and Survival" on Michael Tymn's Blog and a presentation, "Science and Spirituality," reproduced in the *IANDS Journal.*

From among his and others' experiences involving end-of-life research, we learn of many observations about events some dying patients may describe or may even be witnessed by others. These include the following:

• Some people will have a premonition that they will die within two years.

- The dying will be visited by a dead relative nearer to the time of death.
- Dead relatives promise they will be back to pick them up, and perhaps when.
- The dying may be able to negotiate brief postponement of their death.
- Surroundings of love, light, and spiritual beings surround the dying.
- Just before death, paralyzed people sometimes are able to sit up.
- Alzheimer's patients sometimes regain their memory for periods of time.
- The dying may "appear" to loved ones. Distance and time are not factors.
- The dying sometimes see a mirage, sparks, and radiant light.

Soul consciousness separates from and leaves the body at death. As Plato said, "Once free of the body, the soul is able to see truth clearly, because it is more pure than before and recalls the pure ideas which it knew before."

Peter Fenwick also offered the following that seem to qualify more as after-death communications:

- Coincidences that happen around the time of death, involving the appearance of the dying person to a close relative or friend who is not physically present.
- Phenomena that occur around the time of death: such as clocks stopping, strange animal behavior, or lights and equipment turning on and off.
- Not all persons have witnessed the incredible experiences associated with a soul's departure into a different realm during death of the mortal body.
- For those who have, these represent psychic manifestations of the soul's amazing capabilities and perhaps psychic linking with witnesses' souls.

Maggie Callahan and Patricia Kelley, both hospice professionals, published their experiences under the endearing title, *Final Gifts: Understanding the Special Awareness, Needs, and Communications of the Dying.* This is a first-hand collection of stories worth reading about end-of-life events.

In the paper, "Deathbed Observations by Physicians and Nurses," psychologist Karlis Osis studied 640 reports from ten thousand American physicians and nurses about patients' visions as they faced death. These typically occurred in *unsedated* patients, whose minds were clear at the time. Their visions often had characteristics that are common to near-death experiences. Similarly, "shared-death experiences" deal with a variety of extra senses, including telepathy, clairvoyance, and even out-of-body experiences. Pain, experienced earlier, disappeared. Patients spoke of seeing angels, other worlds, or deceased loved ones, and they knew they were dying.

Mists and Spirit Bodies During Death

Raymond Moody and Paul Perry's book, *Glimpses of Eternity: Sharing a Loved One's Passage From This Life to the Next*, was mentioned earlier, describing his and his family's "shared death" experience during the death of his mother. But other "shared death" descriptions from medical personnel, and especially hospice nurses, were not mentioned until now. They are more suitable in this chapter. These seem fitted to the idiom: "must be seen to be appreciated."

- A mist that rises over the body in death.

- A spirit replica of the body gets up and walks away.
- A pillar of light on each side at the head of the bed.
- A spirit replica of the deceased spouse appears to help the dying.
- An out-of-body experience sweeps up a loved one with the dying.

After-Death Communications

These are called by many terms but involve "awareness" at some distance that a loved one has died, sometimes eerily at the moment of death. In his book *Lessons from the Light: What We Can Learn from the Near-Death Experience,* psychologist Kenneth Ring described these as "after-death communications" (ADCs). He said they are probably the single most relevant variety of death-related experience.

Ring also revealed that Bill and Judy Guggenheim "personally amassed more than 3,300 accounts of [such] cases indicative of *real*—not hallucinatory—contact with deceased loved ones. They chose to present about ten percent of these, some 350 stories, in their book *Hello from Heaven: A New Field of Research: After-Death Communication Confirms That Life and Love Are Eternal.*

ADCs are sometimes called grief-induced "hallucinations" by skeptics. But the Guggenheims' case studies include many persons who perceived ADCs from loved ones *before* they were later notified that their loved ones had died.

It is estimated that almost one-third of Americans have experienced an "after-death communication" from a deceased loved one, according to Julie Beischel, director of research at the Windbridge Institute. These manifestations naturally have occurred in a wide variety of ways, and the survivor's realization is conditioned by his or her willingness to accept such phenomena as real. It may be nothing more than the characteristic whiff of the deceased's favorite dinner entrée late in the evening or the hallway grandfather clock stopping at the exact time of the loved one's demise. Yet, why should his or her grieving spouse deny this reminder that love reaches across all borders?

Taboos

Yet, people never discuss *their* deaths. When the topic does arise, it invariably pertains to the deaths of other people. As a result, survivors often are left to deal with legal, financial, and funeral arrangements as well as grief—this can be overwhelming in deaths that were totally unexpected!

The last two weeks of our lives have been called the "most expensive," as family members and even patients demand the most advanced and expensive procedures to delay death. One clergy member suggested that it is more humane for family members to reassure their loved ones that "It's OK to go," rather than "Hang in there!"

Yet dying is still one of our greatest fears, for our selves and for our loved ones. It often is untimely, coming as a shock or after long anxiety. Therefore, grief over the loss of a loved one is always natural—one who is very dear to our hearts, whose *earthly* presence we will see no more. No other demand on our lives seems so traumatic, with its turbulent upheaval in survivors' lives.

New Horizon

But individualism is now challenging the status quo. Apparently more than twenty-two million patients around the world have described their near-death experiences (NDEs). Individual spirituality is being encouraged, with benefits for health as well. Between NDEs and individual spirituality an unusual link exists, which just might infuse funerals with more optimism—a reassurance of reunions with loved ones in Heaven, with everyone looking as they did on Earth but very healthy.

But neither God nor Heaven is likely to be personally accepted as "real" by everyone until our bodies die *and* only when we experience the afterlife firsthand. Yet actual manifestations of fetus' emotional trauma, shared-death experiences, cardiac arrest survivors' testimonies, hypnotic regression accounts, and young children's verified past life accounts—*all* offer *experiential evidence* of souls and soul consciousness.

These details, acquired from thousands of experiences and studies, can be correlated to provide an encouraging promise of our souls' existence *and* its survival of mortal death. This offers a positive step too, toward acknowledging the also-imperceptible reality of God and Heaven.

The next chapter discusses what souls call the "return home."

Chapter Seventeen

Return Home

Toronto ON psychiatrist Joel Whitton therefore stressed that a soul's initial reaction to departing at death of the physical body usually is the same, regardless of the number of its reincarnations. He said that souls typically leave behind any animal instincts affecting them when they depart the human body: "anger, sensual pleasure, lust, sadness, and jealousy." Newton found that "some souls do carry the negative baggage of a difficult past life longer than others." But Newton and Whitton both stressed that soul readjustment to the spirit world depends upon "the soul's level of spiritual growth; its attachment to memories left from this life on earth; and the nature and timing of death."

Newton's description about the spiritual care of each returning soul begins at what is called the "Gateway." Upon exiting the "tunnel," one or more souls of previously departed friends and relatives may be waiting at the "Gateway" to welcome each arriving soul. There is nothing haphazard about those friends or relatives knowing *exactly* when souls are due and where to meet them in the spirit world. This can have an overwhelming impact on many returning souls—seeing previously departed *people* whom the dying *person* may have doubted *ever* seeing again. As implied at the beginning of this chapter, such a meeting also occurs when a sudden cardiac arrest victim "visits Heaven."

At the Gateway to the spirit world, the baggage starts to diminish. The soul soon recognizes the "carefully directed order and harmony" of the "world" it had left for its most recent reincarnation.

Energy Restoration

Human beings have been deprived of knowing about their souls until recently—and many people still are not aware or do not believe. Obviously, therefore, many souls may return home without successful reincarnations. The outcome may even be worse if souls' efforts run afoul of their hosts' self-gratification at other people's misfortunes. If, by chance, the host's penchant for risky ventures attracts its soul's weakness, the soul may lose entirely.

But Heaven is prepared to immediately offer energy repair and restoration, even before meetings with soul guides or the Council. Yet, the potential threats that can emerge during a reincarnation emphasize that, despite each soul's wholehearted commitment to helping its host and learning about human frailties, it may return home "bloodied and battered."

Transition and Placement

Newton's first book spent two chapters on these aspects of souls returning home. This involves gathering and movement of returning souls to rejoin their specific groups in the spirit world. Large numbers of returning souls apparently are conveyed in a spiritual form of mass transit to their proper destinations. Newton comments that an outstanding characteristic of the spirit world is "a continuous feeling of a powerful mental force facilitating everything in uncanny harmony." Perhaps it is obvious by now that the spirit world can address the needs of souls individually and in mass.

Home Colonies

At its intended destination, the returning soul is said to debark the spiritual mass transit at the place reserved for its colony. It is composed of a group of souls at its own level of spiritual advancement. But not *all* of the souls whose *hosts* were our human family members and friends in our just past earthly life are on the same developmental level in Heaven. Yet our departed loved ones will meet us at the Gateway when our soul arrives, looking like they and we did on earth but without infirmities.

Memories of the Past

So *each* soul has immortal memories of *each* human lifetime on Earth and of *each* human family. Naturally, some such memories may be more pleasant than others. Yet the bonds of genuine love reach across the millennia of both Earth and Heaven.

As Jesus said, "There are no marriages in Heaven." But there also is *no* jealousy, envy, or any other *negative* human emotion in Heaven. This helps account for the state of Heavenly relationships among souls that were described earlier.

Remarkably, however, from his research Michael Newton found that "members of the same soul group most definitely choose new families on Earth where they can be together."

This happened among his seven thousand patients and clients in "life-between-lives" hypnotic regression often enough for him to eventually offer a chart of typical group-member arrangements in his book *Destiny of Souls.*

Spirit Guides

Spirit (i.e., soul) guides are assigned to each incarnating soul. The one possible common denominator for all such sources of help might best be called "spirit entities." Reports from Newton's clients account for spirit entities in a variety of roles. One or more—a second would be in training—of these advanced entities seem able to help souls in special ways:

- Watching over incarnated souls.
- Escorting returning souls through the "tunnel."
- Meeting and comforting them at the "Gateway."
- Reorienting returning souls to the spirit world.
- Joining each in its appearance before the council.
- Counseling souls in need of help.
- Assisting them in planning for reincarnation.

One of Newton's hypnotic regression clients said, "We are always protected, supported, and directed within the system by master souls."

Council of Elders

Each soul "returning home" to the spirit world meets one or more times with its "Council of Elders." This group of advanced souls exemplifies empathy and compassion—two traits that souls are expected to master through repeated incarnations on Earth. Each soul has its own council to whom everything about it is totally transparent, so the soul is its own worst critic.

This first meeting is a review of the soul's self-accountability for its most recent incarnation. That appearance before the Council obviously is the one that souls fear most. But each soul knows that this is critical to its growth and development. Later meetings with the Council may help the soul plan its future incarnations in line with its karmic balance sheet and challenges remaining to be mastered.

Individual souls therefore are encouraged to refrain from discussing their council meetings later with other souls—to "block" the participant-soul's thoughts—to maintain privacy. This seems to discourage "second-guessing" by fellow souls.

But council meetings in *no* way imply that "all is forgiven." Rather, souls whose human hosts egregiously and unconscionably mistreated others seem to be offered unusual options. One is to immediately reincarnate in "reverse" circumstances for the host—to experience what its *victims* experienced in the life just past. Another choice is solitary self-isolation for an extended period of time, even for many earth-lifetimes—thus penalizing that soul's progress. Obviously, this is a kind of "hell."

However, when returning souls with minor host infractions from their latest incarnation meet with their councils, council members may consider overwhelming causes for a soul's inability to influence its host's behavior—especially if efforts by the soul are *apparent*.

This may involve the soul's maturity, its progress, and the challenges it faced. Also included, therefore, might be the host's mental state, his or her strengths and weaknesses, and any instinctive human excesses. Any or all of these could influence the host's attitude toward and treatment of others *and* the soul's success or lack of it in influencing its host. However, failure could still require the soul to face the same challenges in a future reincarnation.

Yet, because karma may seem rather strict for souls' self-accountability upon their "return home," council members consider many aspects of the soul, its host, and the nature of their life together. Apparently the soul is well aware that its primary goal is conquering fear of the human condition. This seems necessary in order to grow spiritually by overcoming negative emotions through perseverance over many Earth lifetimes. But this often results in souls returning home bruised and hurt. Still, a soul's failure to master a human frailty may well require it to undergo one or more additional reincarnations during which to overcome that shortcoming.

Also, a word of caution: no one escapes the problems of life on Earth by choosing to end it abruptly. The Council of Elders frowns upon suicide during a healthy life. It too can result in that soul having to relive the same challenges in its next reincarnation.

Yet, on a positive note, council members also compliment souls for their hosts' specific acts of empathy, compassion, or benevolence toward others during their incarnation. Souls may have forgotten such individual instances but these were very evident to the council.

But souls' individual differences give them weaknesses and strengths, like humans. Depending upon the nature of the *mix* of soul and human characteristics in any reincarnation, certain combinations seem more able to work together in successfully avoiding human pitfalls. Yet other mixes may involve negative, sometimes instinctive, human behavior that *attracts* the soul's weakness.

For example, a risk-taking, aggressive, or adventurous soul may become engrossed with its human host's life styles and emotions. Such a soul might become passively involved with a host whose self-esteem feeds on power struggles for material gain without concern for others. That reincarnation could fail to fulfill any of its three purposes. Yet, God never intended to punish—or to have any human religion punish—humankind for its frailties. After all, He also gave us free will.

But the Council of Elders considers suicide by a young healthy person to be a wasted life for a soul and requires the soul to repeat that reincarnation.

The Spirit World

Newton also stressed several principles that apply in the afterlife. First, space there is infinite, something we can't even imagine. Second, despite its population of billions of souls, there is a "structure and order to the spirit world beyond human imagination." Third, the spirit world has unlimited access to energy forces designed to perform various operations more effectively and efficiently than anything that engineers can design on earth.

Newton writes that the ambience there "is a sublime matrix of compassion, harmony, ethics, and morality *far* beyond what we practice on earth." Ubiquitous harmony of spirit, honesty, humor, and love are the primary foundations of the spirit world. Because this is so different from what we know on earth, it may be hard to even imagine.

Various reports from "life-between-lives" spiritual regression subjects, and from near-death survivors, spoke of the spirit world as containing cities of light, spheres, beautiful gardens, fruit, magnificent buildings, homes, clothed entities resembling human form, lectures, study halls, and busy involvement in research, record keeping, and so forth.

But remember that the spirit world is a *real* world powered by the incorporeal energy of thought and home to vast numbers of incorporeal entities, despite how humanly unimaginable that may seem! Also, consider the vast varieties of apparently material objects and creatures that can possibly result from unlimited creative energy.

Near-death survivors who "visit Heaven" speak of "feeling" overwhelming love and of "knowing" their place in the vastness of it all. At some time, NDE victims may "see" beautiful and expansive landscapes with buildings, trees, flowers, and the like. But *none* of the thousands of subjects of spiritual (i.e., life-between-lives) hypnotic regression have *ever* claimed to *see* God.

Earlier in the book, the spirit world was said to be incorporeal (i.e., without material substance and form), like God and our souls. You may recall that Cicoria's details of his near-death experience were very specific. A couple of points he made might even have been overlooked. Although they are not scientific proof in themselves, they might suggest something more worth noting in this chapter. The following italicized excerpts therefore focus on his seemingly cogent points:

> "Once outside, I was *immersed in a bluish white light that had a shimmering appearance as if I were swimming underwater in a crystal clear stream.* The *sunlight was penetrating* through it. The visual was accompanied by *a feeling of absolute love and peace* … That was what I felt; *I had fallen into a pure positive flow of energy. I could see the flow of this energy. I could see it flow through the fabric of everything. I reasoned that this energy was quantifiable. It was something measurable and palpable. As I flowed in the current of this stream, which seemed to have both velocity and direction* … I became ecstatic at the possibility of *where I was going. I was aware of every moment of this experience, conscious of every millisecond, even though I could feel that time did not exist."*

This was brought to your attention as perhaps the *only* time the "spirit world" may have been revealed, perhaps because no other NDE survivor has ever noticed it. Although it is occasionally mentioned in metaphysics, the so-called "spirit world" apparently is *not* humanly perceptible, yet it seems to encompass all of creation. Cicoria said, "*I could see it flow through the fabric of everything.*"

The next chapter is for you, the reader, and your family and friends.

Chapter Eighteen

Mortal Death

This book would be remiss if it failed to address human "survival" of mortal death, sometimes called "the afterlife." Perhaps ironically, the term "mortal" is typically defined as "subject to death." Although this book has a different meaning of "mortal death" than do most health care professionals, it seems uncertain whether religious leaders agree with this book.

So this chapter appears here rather than earlier in the book, to offer the reader an *opportunity* to become familiar with this book's conviction about survival of our God-given soul and its remarkable immortal whole life memory of its human host in each incarnation of every soul that ever reincarnates on Earth.

Usual Impact

Naturally, each of us has one or more loved ones and friends whose deaths we mourned. Grief came whether their departure was unexpected or imminent. Our fond memories remain, even though we may never expect to share those with them again. But this book emphasizes that a vital part of each of us *does* survive, including our memories.

Yet, people never discuss *their* deaths. When the topic does arise, it invariably pertains to the deaths of other people. As a result, survivors often are left to deal with legal, financial, and funeral arrangements as well as grief. Physicians and nurses used to be forbidden to even mention "death" or "dying." The subject still remains taboo in many cases, felt to represent a treatment failure.

Furthermore, the last two weeks of our lives has been called the "most expensive," as family members and even patients demand the most advanced and expensive procedures to delay death. However, one clergy member suggested that it is more humane for family members to reassure their loved ones that "It's OK to go," rather than "Hang in there!"

Human religions usually treat death as final, sometimes tinged with Christianity's sting of original sin, hell, or purgatory. The promise of reunions in Heaven with departed loved ones is ignored as if it never exists.

Yet, all of us naturally are concerned, too, about our own individual outlook. Is physical death as final as atheists or other skeptics may insist? NDE survivors who "visited Heaven" know otherwise.

Our Soul's Concern

After spending a human lifetime with its host, and if the union was amicable, Michael Newton assures us that our soul will be especially sensitive to our surviving loved one's grief. Newton's spiritual regression (i.e., "life-between-lives") clients' souls typically exemplify this following the host's death scene before returning to Heaven. With its unlimited psychic capabilities, the soul usually tries to comfort surviving loved ones.

Yet spouses, who have an uncanny sensation that reminds them of their recently deceased loved one,rrd seldom tell anyone else, for fear of being considered weird. Yet, spouses who *fail* to experience this may simply have refused to accept that it is possible. Bonds of love seem able to reach across distance and time, since these are not from the grave but from the eternal spirit world.

You may have heard of so-called "mediums" that apparently have a special sensitivity to "spiritual" messages from the departed to loved ones on Earth. Some mediums have had near-death experiences, too, which may account for this ability. James Van Praagh, for example, describes his NDE in his new book, *Adventures of the Soul.* His book also discusses human vibrations, which were detailed in Valerie Hunt's classic book *Infinite Mind: Science of the Human Vibrations of Consciousness,* mentioned earlier in this book. Van Praagh says that he must elevate his vibrations to receive messages from departed loved ones' souls.

You may feel disappointed that the part of each of us that seems to survive death of the material body is our soul's complete immortal memory of our life. But remember, too, that our soul's immortal memory contains everyone who was part of our life, all memories of our lives together, as well as with our pets. Apparently, too, our soul can develop a special affinity for our family members and pets.

Our Future

When our soul returns to Heaven after our mortal death, we now can expect its experience to be similar to that of the sudden cardiac arrest victim "visiting Heaven." One difference does seem possible, however—Heaven will know whether our soul will stay and it will plan appropriately for our soul's "arrival." This includes reunions with our departed loved ones and, later, additional reunions with loved ones we left behind when their souls join ours in Heaven.

Of course, many sudden cardiac arrest victims are resuscitated *before* their souls can "visit Heaven." So their souls *often* remain near the ceiling of the emergency room, watching the medical team working on their bodies below. But remember Tony Cicoria's "just a ball of energy and thought" and Katie "wandered through her home." Detached from its host's "dead" body, the soul can travel anywhere—including Heaven, as during NDEs from sudden cardiac arrest.

Also, it now seems likely that the soul's immortal lifetime memory of the single personality shared between the soul and its host is what each soul carries with it to Heaven. Remember that near-death survivors claimed that "the *real me* "was what separated with their soul during sudden cardiac arrest. Likewise, the spirit world will make certain that the souls of previously deceased loved ones and friends will know so that reunions can be planned—such as Don Piper described.

In addition, remember from an earlier chapter the "women" that came into Kubler-Ross' and the author's lives, and the latter one stayed more than a year! These seem to illustrate each soul's creative ability, for itself and for its hosts.

Souls acknowledge that they *cannot* bring their entire energy into a single incarnation, since it would "blow the human brain apart." Part of each soul's energy therefore always remains in Heaven. If nothing more, please realize that God's "spirit world" is absolutely beyond every human's imagination and comprehension! Its unconditional love and our human love reach beyond all boundaries.

Sensing Loved Ones Again on Earth

This topic heading will seem absurd—until you have accepted the plausibility of the contents of this book about souls and reincarnation. But it is included for those readers who may already have an appreciation for the special nuances of the spirit world.

Considering several points may help:

• Human beings do not have multiple lives like souls.
• Souls often reincarnate as a group, in human bodies of friends or relatives.
• Some young people can recall their soul's previous life and family members.
• That ability fades with age.
• A sixth sense about someone's traits may remind us of a departed love one.

Michael Newton's claim in his first book supports this: "Those who have just died are not devastated about their death, because they *know* those left of Earth will see them again in the spirit world *and probably later in other lives as well.*" Of course, remember how this happens for souls.

So Newton's Spiritual and Human Genealogy chart in his second book illustrates interrelationships among twenty-four different people (e.g., relatives and friends), who each represent an individual soul incarnation. Yet he emphasizes that such "soul families" do *not* incarnate in the same hereditary family they had in past lives, in order to learn new lessons. But considering that the group may be of different ages, this might be an innocent question from a two-year-old boy to his mother: "Mommy, remember when I was your daddy?" Nevertheless, this discussion might prompt readers to wonder about their families and friends now on Earth.

Spiritualism

Spiritualism was a religious movement that developed in England and reached its peak growth both there and in the United States from the 1840s to the 1920s. It held the belief that the spirits of the dead exist in a so-called afterlife, and they have the inclination and ability to communicate with the dead. This discussion is included as full disclosure, just as James Van Praagh was mentioned earlier in this chapter, since books on these subjects continue to be popular.

In this country, spiritualism got a boost in 1848 when two daughters found that they could "communicate" with strange "raps" in the old house, apparently from the "spirit" of a person murdered and apparently buried under the house five years earlier. Human remains were discovered five feet down. This and the following were excerpted from Michael Tymns' book, *The Afterlife Revealed.*

Early psychical researchers claimed that the soul leaves the body soon after its physical death. Yet a "spirit body" lingers for some time, also called a "double, etheric, or astral" body, among other names. Its "survival" destination is said to depend upon the kind of life the person lived on Earth.

Now you realize that so-called "mortal death" is *not* final. But before the final chapter on relationships with your soul, has this book in *any* way prompted you to reconsider your life on Earth? The next chapter has some thoughts.

Chapter Nineteen

What Is the Meaning of It All?

Since human religions—and secular beliefs—account for much of our human attitudes and behavior, it seems worthwhile to examine why. Consider these thoughts:

- What is the meaning of existence? Why are there pain and death? What is life really all about and what is its object? Why *not* live for maximum personal gratification?
- These are not just questions that people ask *after* they have managed (or failed) to achieve their goals.
- But these questions drive our behavior daily in our careers, professions, and family matters.
- And they unconsciously control our attitudes and behavior toward *other* people.

Yet, remember the conversions that NDE survivors bring back from "visiting Heaven":

- Much greater appreciation for life itself.
- Deeper sense of wonder and gratitude about living.
- Greater self-esteem and self-confidence.
- Compassion and understanding for everyone.
- Stronger reverence for life in all of its forms.
- Disavowal of competitive and materialistic pressures.
- Caring and concern for others.
- Personal certainty about the existence of God.
- No longer fear death.

This chapter therefore stands on its own. The author did not contrive it. Yet it is reminiscent of the authenticity with which we *all* were born, despite our ethnicity, color of our skin, social standing, wealth, education, or any other human characteristic or trait. We all are united through our God-given souls.

Remember Kenneth Ring's observation about such survivor transformations:

"If we accept the truth of the NDE's chief revelation, it can only be that we have lost touch with the Source. Essentially we have fallen out of Love … and have forgotten our true home. Since Love is the essential truth of the NDE, it can also set us free."

This book implies the significance of love in our lives on Earth, but without specific details. The book also has emphasized the role of energy in various applications. Yet, very few readers likely could ever imagine that love itself *is* energy! Of course, from what you have read in this book, it may have occurred to you that God may be our Source of love energy, too. So the next chapter will at least amaze, if not shock, you at the *power* of love, given and received!

Chapter Twenty

The Energy of Love

Magic or Science?

Love has always been considered a significant source of energy and emotion by bards and poets. Now science has proved this to be fact rather than fiction.

Incredibly, love can change water into the most beautiful ice crystals. A Japanese scientist, Masaro Emoto, made a marvelous contribution to the world of energy. Bradley Nelson's book described Emoto's research into the crystalline structure of water, i.e., crystalline structures formed by frozen water droplets. It was detailed in the scientist's book *The Hidden Messages in Water.*

Emoto found that water would form various patterns of "snowflakes" when exposed to different influences. Acid rock music, for example, would result in a very disrupted crystal. A Mozart symphony would provide a beautifully formed crystal. The most "intensely beautiful ice crystals" emerged after water's overnight exposure to the phrase "Love and Gratitude." This could be done by the effort of writing the words on a piece of paper and taping them to the container. Writing and attaching "I hate you" produced an "asymmetrical and disrupted crystal."

In another experiment, Emoto sealed cooked rice in three jars. He then entrusted each jar to a separate group of school children. For the first jar children were told to say pleasant words to it. For the second jar kids were to say harsh words to it. Children were requested to ignore the third jar. Checking all three jars a few weeks later, Emoto found the rice in the first jar as fresh as the day it had been sealed. Rice in the second jar had some mold. But the rice in the third jar was completely rotten.

Intention and Perception

Love existed in the minds of both the giver and the receiver, so to speak, as does its absence. Love's span of existence extends from family and friends to strangers, ranging from nurturing to total disregard. Often surprisingly, strangers volunteer concern and care for those virtually unknown victims of sudden hardship or disaster. So love is often better interpreted and understood in terms of soul attributes like empathy, compassion, and benevolence.

Love Not Restricted to Humans

As incredible as Emoto's results were, there seemed to be strikingly similar results reported in Lynne McTaggart's book. In her book, she described a lengthy series of experiments conducted by Cleve Backster, the country's leading lie-detector expert.

Lie detectors are sensitive to the slightest change in electrical conductivity of skin, as well as blood pressure, respiration, and pulse rates. For thirty years, Backster experimented in measuring humanly imperceptible changes in plants by connecting them to lie-detector devices and registering plant changes on that equipment. His results defied explanation for the longest time, during which he endured ridicule by conventional scientists.

Initially, he found that plants exhibited their response according to their perception of his intentions: showing a pair of cutters produced a threat response; a perceived supportive intention produced opposite results. He even found that plants would respond to perceived threats to other life forms. Pouring boiling water into a sink drain surprised him with their negative response until he discovered living microbes in the sink drainpipe. Dumping brine shrimp into boiling water could elicit a negative response from the plants even if the act was committed in a distant room.

A clincher occurred when Backster and his partner set up an ingenious time- switch device whereby the shrimp could be dumped into the boiling water later, after the two humans left the premises and were unaware of the act at the time it happened. The plants reflected the threat at the time it occurred.

Rupert Sheldrakes' research showed that dogs could register anticipation of their owners' intentions to take them for a walk. Sheldrake described this in his book *The Sense of Being Stared At and Other Unexplained Powers of the Human Mind*. This occurred with the dogs in separate enclosures, being videotaped with a hidden camera, and with the owners simply *thinking* about walking them.

Pre-Birth Communications

This subject likely will stretch people's imagination or provoke outright disbelief. To some extent it falls into the same genre as pre-life planning, reincarnation, and psychic and mystical experiences that were explored elsewhere in this book. The closest subjective experience is precognition, having a vision of future events. Pre-birth visions or sensations about yet-to-be-born children apparently are not uncommon.

Underlying all of the personal accounts from parents-to-be about pre-birth communications is a common theme: the energy of love. If love is indeed a spiritual energy, it must have been the force that facilitated these case reports. One of the best collections of such first-hand stories is Sarah Hinze's book *We Lived in Heaven: Spiritual Accounts of Souls Coming to Earth*.

Author Elisabeth Hallett wrote about this in her online article "The Mystery of Pre-Birth Communication." Although many prospective parents are having these experiences, most seem reluctant to mention them. Both parents-to-be may have the same dream. But if one spouse does and the other doesn't, it could introduce a suspicion of disbelief.

Hallett said that these experiences may be only subtle feelings or vivid life-like dreams. Typically, the feelings actually may occur before conception, while the dreams seem more likely during pregnancy. These communications occasionally seem to take the form of messages, particularly when the prospective mother may be worried about the safety of her fetus. Even though such pre-birth revelations naturally surprise any parent- to-be, the sensation is said to represent such a warm expression of love and bonding that it becomes a great reassurance to future parents.

Hallett also wrote *Soul Trek: Meeting our Children on the Way to Birth* and *In the Newborn Year: Our Changing Awareness After Childbirth*. Another book related to this subject is Eliot Jay Rosen's *Experiencing the Soul: Before Birth, During Life, After Death*.

David Larsen examined such reports in his Latter Day Saint (LDS) Weblog "Heavenly Ascent." He quoted John Denver's and Richard Dreyfuss's testimonies regarding their experiences in pre-birth communications. Larsen also claims "Over 800 references to the pre-earth existence of mankind have been identified in Jewish and Christian sources from the time of Christ until the sixth century AD. Early Hellenistic (Greek) writings also referred to belief in a pre-earth life." The LDS.net blog also has personal posts on "What Kids Remember About the Pre-Existence."

There are a number of online first-hand accounts from prospective parents about their pre-birth communication experiences. One is Theresa Danna's "Pre-Birth Communication: The Link Of Love." For readers interested in books on this subject, go to http://www.light-hearts.com/treasury.htm. For letters from parents describing their pre- birth communications, go to http://www.light-hearts.com/letters.htm. For articles, try http://www.light-hearts.com/articles.htm.

From Case Files

John James's book tells of a case from the files of Massachusetts General Hospital. A well-known photo entitled "The Rescuing Hug" supports it. "Souls of twins," James wrote, "are known for their very close connections." The hospital staff felt that one twin would die. Each was in a separate incubator, as hospital policy required. Nurse Kasparian ignored orders and placed both in the same incubator.

Instantly the two snuggled together. The stronger one put her arm across her sister and held her close. The weaker one calmed her breathing to that of her sister's pace and both survived. James concluded, "Simply experiencing touch and sharing energies made her [the weaker twin] stronger."

Energy Bond

Gwendolyn Jones's book *A Cry from the Womb: Healing the Heart of the World: A Guide to Healing and Helping Souls Return to the Light After Sudden Death, Miscarriage, Stillbirth or Abortion* is another example of the power of the energy of love. It deals more specifically with sudden death, miscarriage, stillbirth, and abortion, with regard to their effect on the soul of a fetus or baby. Like pre-birth communications, this book attests to the sensory bond between incarnating souls and host parents, particularly the mother. Jones's book suggests that the energy of love creates a parent-child bond sometimes even before conception, one that survives even death of the physical body.

Finally, the chapter is next that hopefully enables each reader to establish a mutually beneficial relationship with his or her soul.

Chapter Twenty-One

Messages From Our Souls

From earlier discussions, you may have surmised that most people's pace of living involves a dominant left hemisphere. You might even think that any sense of urgency from our soul in our right hemisphere might likely be shut out, and routine assistance from our soul should not even be expected.

So perhaps the *only* way you *might* accept that you *actually* have a soul is *if* and *when* you "sense" it. Naturally, this is *not* by any of your five human senses: see, touch, hear, taste, or smell. Moreover, you will *never* be *consciously* aware of your soul as part of your "waking consciousness."

Rather, that "sense" likely will come simply "out of the blue," so to speak—an unusual, unexpected, and subtle *feeling*. It may seem to suggest: "try something you have not considered," "what to do in an *unusual* situation," or even "don't!" in what seems like a *normal* situation. What it likely *will* be recommending is *not* what you typically would expect to do!

No doubt many people have had such a feeling. But most might just ignore it as "odd." Yet, as discussed earlier in the book, some people *are* familiar with experiences called "gut feelings," "hunches," or even the more sophisticated "intuition."

Remember Professor Gerd Gigerenzer's book *Gut Feelings: The Intelligence of the Unconscious.* He believes that "gut feelings," "intuition," and "hunches" appear simply as an unusual feeling. Notably, he names "the unconscious" (i.e., right hemisphere)—implicitly the soul—as the source.

Examples

One of these "suggestions" that the author recently experienced is a good example. He was replacing a very small battery in a hearing aid but it accidentally got caught on an angle rather than drop snugly into its compartment. It seemed impossible to remove and correct it, leaving him puzzled and frustrated. Soon he "felt" a "suggestion," very strange because it didn't make normal sense to him. "Open the drawer in that table and look at the back side of the battery compartment." There in the drawer was a package of round-headed brass paper fasteners (i.e., "brads"), each with two long thin, flat "nails" hanging down. Checking further, he found that the *back* side of the battery compartment had an open slit in the middle, perfect for inserting one of the "nails" to dislodge the battery! Eureka! The author then remembered buying the fasteners years ago, but he never knew where he had stored them!

For another example, the author was driving on a two-lane road late one dark night. Both sides of the road were heavy with trees and shrubs. He had been talking with passengers. Suddenly, thoughts about deer just popped into his mind. "What?" he wondered. Yet, he slowed the van. Soon, twenty feet ahead, a couple of deer emerged from the overgrowth to cross the road. Others slowly followed, the last being a fawn—for which he had to brake sharply!

Everyday Matters

So consider that your *soul's* consciousness may have the same concerns that you have, even if you don't realize you have a soul or know what a "soul" is. But the soul retains its special capabilities that enable it to have a much different *perspective* from yours. In the two examples from the author, his soul's consciousness seemed to "see" what he could not see and even "know" the future.

So consider Newton's comment: "While soul memory may be hidden from the level of conscious awareness through amnesia [i.e., veil of forgetfulness], thought patterns of the soul influence the human brain to induce motivations for certain actions."

Considerations

There are aspects of everyone's lives that might be considered to enhance sensitivity and receptivity to soul influences and to encourage them:

• Trust your feelings, being cautious of nagging or uncomfortable feelings.
• Think back to similar past situations. Try to take a neutral position now.
• Emotional needs, fears, desires, and expectations can interfere.
• Impulsivity is counterproductive.
• May be concerned with safety and welfare of you and your loved ones.
• Assistance may depend on its effect on others.
• Humility and gratitude for help seem to encourage it.
• Be in the present moment, not worrying about yesterday or tomorrow.

The author admits how difficult it is for him to maintain these ideals. For example, we likely analyze situations and rationalize the answers *we* want or could reasonably expect. But since soul messages seem to come "out of the blue," he has adopted a simple slogan to often remind himself, "Be *here* now!"

So we might *first* become aware of soul messages because of the nature of their *content*. Remember, our souls have a perspective of both seen and unseen physical and non-physical reality—present and future—more than any information available to us. Possible examples include premonitions of a potential accident or danger; a concern for loved ones; or a suggestion for the location of a lost item or the solution to a problem.

Receptivity

Nancy Rosanoff's classic book *Intuition Workout: A Practical Guide to Discovering and Developing Your Inner Knowing* provides a series of exercises to make people more comfortable and effective in developing their intuition. She has conducted training classes for corporations, universities, and other groups for many years. Rosanoff stressed that intuition cannot be forced. However, we can learn to focus our concerns, questions, and decisions in such a way that they *invite* intuition.

One commonality among gut feelings, hunches, and intuition therefore seems to be the need to release ourselves from the typical constraints of our left cerebral hemisphere: logical, rational, and analytical. In other words, be able to *also* think—or even loosen up our concentration—in ways that invite gut feelings, hunches, intuition, *or soul messages*—whatever you call "it."

Morning Pages

Writing and periodically reviewing is a useful technique for all manner of purposes, including "felt" messages. Author Janet Conner tried a version called "morning pages" during her painful divorce. She said this "worked miracles." Conner's positive results led to her book *Writing Down Your Soul: How to Activate and Listen to the Extraordinary Voice Within.* Conner's Web site (www.janetconner.com) illustrates that she apparently struck a responsive chord with many people. She has published several books, conducts courses, and has a radio show called "The Soul-Directed Life." Ironically, the topic for one show was "The Call to Become Friends With Death."

Soul Messages

Each of us seems able to cultivate a relationship with our soul whereby we invite *and* honor soul messages in the intent in which they are offered—to help improve our lives on earth—to find *real* meaning, if you will. It obviously is difficult to give examples of soul messages since they seem intended only for the host, the time, and the situation. As you might expect, however, there are principles for inviting and recognizing soul messages, including:

- Freely given, without demands.
- Patient and understanding.
- Offered in the spirit of empathy and compassion.
- Never for selfish purposes.
- Encouraged by acknowledgment and respect.

Perhaps one of the best examples of "following your gut" seems to have happened during Amateur Night at the Harlem Opera House many years ago. A skinny, awkward sixteen-year-old girl prepares to go fearfully on stage. She is announced to the crowd as a dancer. Then, moments before she appears, the announcer says she has decided to sing instead. Three encores and first prize later, Ella Fitzgerald was history.

Meet Your Soul

The point therefore is to suggest a direction for our lives on earth rather than an overnight goal. Perhaps we could start by taking a few steps toward becoming more "aware" of those around us. Including others "on our radar," so to speak, will help get our souls more involved in our free will choices and actions.

In his second book, Michael Newton writes, "Something within you lying dormant is awakened … your soul flirts with you at first … the attraction of self-discovery begins with an almost playful touching of your consciousness by your unconscious mind. As the intensity of wanting to fully possess our inner Self grows, we are drawn irresistibly into a more intimate relationship. The fascinating aspect about self-discovery is that when you hear that inner voice you instantly recognize it."

Remember that your soul wants to help you, particularly in your relationships with others—therein lies our greatest potential for human frailties:

• Sincerity is easiest to practice with your loved ones, whether caring, listening, complimenting, respecting, or agreeing.

• An argument requires two persons and is most easily prevented or reconciled if one is willing to honestly consider the other's viewpoint.

• Behind every person is a unique story yearning to be heard … and often worth listening to.

• Each of us would love to have others understand us, but we must be willing to understand them too.

• Saying "Good Morning (or Afternoon)" even to a stranger costs us nothing but may help him or her feel "Somebody knows I exist!"

• Passing along compliments or assistance to other people, such as you have received, helps keep kindliness alive.

These may seem simplistic, but your good intentions will become evident and are the catalysts for magic results for others. The reason is that others may overlook how you act or even forgive what you say, but they will never forget *how you made them feel!* This was paraphrased from Maya Angelou, the noted American author and poet.

As you contemplate this chapter, you may find the allusions in the timeless poem *Desiderata* suggestive of its words, "Keep peace with your soul."

The following seems in keeping with the preceding discussion:

Go placidly amid the noise and haste, and remember what peace there may be in silence.

As far as possible without surrender, be on good terms with all persons.

Speak your truth quietly and clearly, and listen to others, even the dull and the ignorant: they too have their story.

Avoid loud and aggressive persons: they are vexations to the spirit.

If you compare yourself with others, you may become vain and bitter; for always there will be greater and lesser persons than yourself.

Enjoy your achievements as well as your plans; keep interested in your own career, however humble; it is a real possession in the changing fortunes of time.

Exercise caution in your business affairs; for the world is full of trickery.

But let this not blind you to what virtue there is; many persons strive for high ideals; and everywhere life is full of heroism.

Be yourself; especially, do not feign affection.

Neither be cynical about love; for in the face of all aridity and disenchantment, it is as perennial as the grass.

Take kindly the counsel of the years, gracefully surrendering the things of youth.

Nurture strength of spirit to shield you in sudden misfortune.

But do not distress yourself with dark imaginings; many fears are born of fatigue and loneliness.

Beyond a wholesome discipline, be gentle with yourself.

You are a child of the universe, no less than the trees and stars; you have a right to be here.

And whether or not it is clear to you, no doubt the universe is unfolding as it should.

Therefore be at peace with God, whatever you conceive Him to be.

And whatever your labors and aspirations, in the noisy confusion about life, keep peace with your soul.

With all its sham, drudgery, and broken dreams, it is still a beautiful world.

Be cheerful.

Strive to be happy.

Max Ehrmann, 1952

Bibliography

American Museum of Natural History. "Black Smokers." http://www.amnh.org/learn/pd/earth/gallery_week6/rfl_index.html

Ars Technica. "*Understanding the Brain* is a catalog of all we don't know about the brain." https://arstechnica.com/science/2018/11/understanding-the-brain-is-a-catalog-of-all-we-dont-know-about-the-brain/

Bache, Christopher M. *Lifecycles: Reincarnation and the Web of Life.* New York, NY: Paragon House, 1994.

Bargh, John and Ezequiel Morsella. 2008. "The Unconscious Mind." *Perspectives on Psychological Science.* yale.edu/acmelab/articles/Bargh_Morsella_Unconscious_Mind.pdf

Beischel, Julie. 2014. "Assisted After-Death Communication: A Self-Prescribed Treatment for Grief." *Journal of Near-Death Studies* 32:3.

Berg, Yahuda. *God Does Not Create Miracles—You Do!*: Los Angeles, CA, Kabbalah Publishing, 2005.

Bowman, Carol. *Children's Past Lives: How Past Life Memories Affect Your Child.* New York, NY: Bantam Books, 1998.

————. *Return from Heaven: Beloved Relatives Reincarnated Within Your Family.* New York, NY: HarperTorch, 2003.

Bullard, David. "Allan Schore on the Science of the Art of Psychotherapy," psychotherapy.net, https://www.psychotherapy.net/interview/allan-schore-neuroscience-psychotherapy

Bussanich, John. "Rebirth Eschatology in Plato and Plotinus," pp. 243-288, in *Philosophy and Salvation in Greek Religion,* ed. Vishwa Adluri, De Gruyter, 2013.

Callahan, Maggie and Patricia Kelley. *Final Gifts: Understanding the Special Awareness, Needs, and Communications of the Dying.* New York, NY: Bantam Dell, 2008.

Cameron, Julie. *The Artist's Way.* New York, NY: Putnam, 2002.

Carroll, Roz. "An Interview with Allan Schore – 'the American Bowlby'." www.thinkbody.co.uk/papers/interview-with-allan-s.htm

Catholic Encyclopedia. "Soul." www.catholic.org/encyclopedia/view.php?id=10963

Centers for Disease Control and Prevention (CDC). *Guide to Understanding Evidence.*

https://www.cdc.gov/violenceprevention/pdf/understanding_evidence-a.pdf

Chamberlain, David. *Babies Remember Birth: And Other Extraordinary Scientific Discoveries About the Mind and Personality of Your Newborn.* Los Angeles, CA: Jeremy P. Tarcher, 1988.

———. 2012. "One Well-Hidden Secret of Good Parenting."
http://dbchamberlainphd.com/2012/12/19/one-well-hidden-secret-of-good-parenting/

———. *Windows to the Womb: Revealing the Conscious Baby from Conception to Birth.* Berkeley, CA: North Atlantic Books, 2013.

Chiron, C. et al. 1997. "The Right Brain Hemisphere is Dominant in Human Infants." NCBI. PubMed.gov. http://www.ncbi.nlm.nih.gov/pubmed/9217688

Chopra, Deepak. *How to Know God.* St. James, MO: Three Rivers, 2000

Cicoria, Anthony. "My Near-Death Experience: A Telephone Call From God."
Missouri Medicine. 111:4:304. July/August 2014.
http://www.omagdigital.com/article/Getting+Comfortable+With+Near-
Death+Experiences/1783389/0/article.html

Conner, Janet. *Writing Down Your Soul: How to Activate and Listen to the Extraordinary Voice Within.* San Francisco, CA: Conari Press, 2009.

Cozolino, Louis. *The Neuroscience of Human Relationships: Attachment and the Developing Social Brain.* New York, NY: Norton, 2006.

Cranston, Sylvia. *Reincarnation: The Phoenix Fire Mystery.* Pasadena, CA: Theosophical University Press, 1998.

David, H.P., Z. Dytrych, and V. Schuller. 1988. "Born Unwanted: Developmental Effects of Denied Abortion. " Avicenum, Prague: Czechoslovak Medical Press.

Danna, Theresa. "Pre-Birth Communication: The Link of Love." Global Oneness.
http://www.experiencefestival.com/a/Pre-BirthCommunication/id/21857.

Dowling, John E. *Creating the Mind: How the Brain Works.* New York, NY: W. W. Norton & Company, 1998.

Dowling, John E. *Understanding the Brain: From Cells to Behavior to Cognition.* New York, NY: W. W. Norton & Company

Eagleman, David. *Incognito: The Secret Lives of the Brain.* New York, NY: Vintage Books, 2012.

———. *The Brain: The Story of You.* New York, NY: Vintage Books, 2017.

Ehrman, Bart. *God's Problem: How the Bible Fails to Answer Our Most Important Question— Why We Suffer*. New York, NY: HarperOne. 2008.

Emoto, Masaro. *The Hidden Messages in Water*. New York, NY: Atria. 2005.

Feldmar, Andrew. "The Embryology of Consciousness: What is a Normal Pregnancy?" *The Psychosocial Aspects of Abortion*. Eds. D. Mall and W. Watts. Washington, DC: University Publications of America, 1979.

Fenwick, Peter and Elizabeth Fenwick. *Art of Dying*. New York, NY: Bloomsbury Academic, 2008.

Fenwick, Peter, Hiliary Lovelace, and Sue Brayne. "Comfort for the Dying: Five Year Retrospective and One Year Prospective Studies of End of Life Experiences." *Archives of Gerontology and Geriatrics*. 2010 Sep-Oct; 51(2); 173-9.

Feynman, Richard. *The Meaning of It All: Thoughts of a Citizen-Scientist*. New York, NY: Basic, 1998.

Frattaroli, Elio. *Healing the Soul in the Age of the Brain:Becoming Conscious in an Unconscious World*. New York, NY, Viking Penguin, 2001

Gershom, Rabbi Yonassan and John Rossner. *Beyond the Ashes: Cases of Reincarnation from the Holocaust*. Virginia Beach, VA: A. R. E. Press, 1992.

Gershom, Rabbi Yonassan. *From Ashes to Healing: Mystical Encounters with the Holocaust*. Virginia Beach, VA: A. R. E. Press, 1996.

Ghasemiannejad, Alinaghi. "Iranian Shiite Muslim Near-Death Experiences: Features and After-Effects Including Dispositional Gratitude." *Journal of Near-Death Studies*: 33(1).

Gigerenzer, Gerd. *Gut Feelings: The Intelligence of the Unconscious*. New York, NY: Penguin Books, 2008.

Gladwell, Malcolm. *Blink: The Power of ThinkingWithout Thinking*. New York, NY: Back Bay Books, 2007

Greyson, Bruce. 2015. "Greyson NDE Scale." IANDS. http://iands.org/research/nde-research/important-research-articles/698-greyson-nde-scale.html

Grosz, Elizabeth. *The Incorporeal: Ontology, Ethics, and the Limits of Materialism*. Columbia University Press: New York, NY, 2017.

Guggenheim, Bill and Judy Guggenheim. *Hello from Heaven: a New Field of Research After-Death Communication Confirms That Life and Love Are Eternal*. New York, NY: Bantam Books, 1997.

Hallett, Elisabeth. 2009. "The Mystery of Pre-Birth Communication."
www.thelaboroflove.com/forum/elisabeth/prebirth.html.

———. *In the Newborn Year: Our Changing Awareness After Childbirth.* Summertown, TN:
Book Publishing Company. 1992.
170
———. *Soul Trek: Meeting Our Children on the Way to Birth.* Hamilton, MT: Light Hearts
Publishing. 1995.

Havel, Vaclav. 1994. "The Need for Transcendence in the Postmodern World."
http://www.worldtrans.org/whole/havelspeech.html.

Henriques, Gregg. 2011. "What Is the Mind? Understanding mind and consciousness via the
unified theory." *Psychology Today.* https://www.psychologytoday.com/us/blog/theory-
knowledge/201112/what-is-the-mind

Hinze, Sarah. *We Lived in Heaven: Spiritual Accounts of Souls Coming to Earth.* Provo, UT:
Spring Creek Book Company 2006.

Hunt, Valerie. *Infinite Mind: Science of the Human Vibrations of Consciousness.* Malibu, CA:
Malibe Publishing Company, 1989.

IANDS. *Journal of Near-Death Studies.* International Association for Near-Death Studies.
Durham, NC.

James, John. *The Great Field: Soul at Play in a Conscious Universe.* Fulton, CA: Elite Books,
2007.

James, William. *Varieties of Religious Experience.* Longman. 1902

Jaynes, Julian. "Consciousness and the Voices of the Mind." McMaster-Bauer Symposium on
Consciousness. *Canadian Psychology.* April, 1986, Vol. 27 (2). Reprinted

Jones, Gwendolyn. *A Cry from the Womb: Healing the Heart of the World: A Guide to Healing
and Helping Souls Return to the Light After Sudden Death, Miscarriage, Stillbirth or Abortion.*
New Braunfels, TX: Angels of Light and Healing. 2004.

Joseph, Rhawn. "Right Brain Unconscious Awareness." *Brain Mind.com.*
http://brainmind.com/RightBrainAwareness.html

Kubler-Ross, Elisabeth. *on LIFE after DEATH.* Berkeley, CA: Ten Speed Press, 2008.

Lagercrantz, Hugo and Jean-Pierre Changeux. "The Emergence of Human Consciousness: From
Fetal to Neonatal Life." IPRF. International Pediatric Research
Foundation. http://www.nature.com/pr/journal/v65/n3/full/pr200950a.html.

Larsen, David. "Heavenly Ascents." 2008. http://www.heavenlyascents.com/2008/08/07/we-lived-in-heaven-sarah-hinze-on-pre- birth-experiences/

Laszlo, Ervin, Stanislav Grof, and Peter Russell. The Consciousness Revolution. Las Vegas, NV: Elf Rock. 2003.

Lehndorff, H. and L. Falkenstein. "Christian Heinrich Heinekin: The Miracle Baby from Lubeck." *Archives of Pediatrics* 72 (1955): 360-377.

Lorenz, Hendrik, "Ancient Theories of Soul", The Stanford Encyclopedia of Philosophy (Summer 2009 Edition), Edward N. Zalta (ed.) http://plato.stanford.edu/archives/sum2009/entries/ancient-soul

MacGregor, Geddes. *Reincarnation in Christianity: A New Vision of the Role of Rebirth in Christian Thought.* Wheaton, IL: Quest Books, 1978.

Mann, Charles C. "The Birth of Religion." *National Geographic* 219: 6.

Maslow, A. H. (1956). Self-actualizing people: A study of psychological ealth. In C. E. Monstakes (Ed.), *The Self: Explorations in Personal Growth*, pp. 160-194. New York: Harper & Row.

Max-Planck-Gesellschaft. 2008. "Unconscious Decisions in the Brain." https://www.mpg.de/research/unconscious-decisions-in-the-brain

McCarty, Wendy Anne. *Welcoming Consciousness: Supporting Babies' Wholeness From the Beginning of Life.* Santa Barbara, CA: Wondrous Beginnings, 2009. . http://www.scientificamerican.com/article.cfm?id=when-does-consciousness-arise

————. Interview with Wendy Anne McCarty, by Kate White. questia. https://www.questia.com/library/journal/1P3-3922023331/interview-with-wendy-anne-mccarty-phd-rn-hnb-bc

McGilchrist, Iain. *The Master and His Emissary: The Divided Brain and the Making of the Western World.* London, England: Yale University Press, 2009.

McTaggart, Lynne. *The Field: The Quest for the Secret Force of the Universe.* New York, NY: HarperCollins, 2002.

————. *The Intention Experiment: Using Your Thoughts to Change Your Life and the World.* New York, NY: Free Press, 2007.

Mendizza, Michael. *Touch the Future: Discovering the Mind of the Prenate.* http://ttfuture.org/store/prenate_mind

Monaghan, F.J. 1980. "Hypnosis in Criminal Investigation." National Criminal Justice Reference Service. www.ncjrs.gov/App/publications/Abstract.aspx?id=70940

Moore, Edward. Origen of Alexandria. *Internet Encyclopedia of Philosophy* (2006). St. Elias School of Orthodox Theology. http://www.iep.utm.edu/o/origen.htm#SH3b.

Moody, Raymond and Paul Perry. *Glimpses of Eternity: Sharing a Loved One's Passage From This Life to the Next.* New York, NY: Guideposts, 2010

Mossberg, Julia A., et al. 2014. "Predicting the Unpredictable: Critical Analysis and Practical Implications of Predictive Anticipatory Activity." *Frontiers in Human Neuroscience.* http://journal.frontiersin.org/article/10.3389/fnhum.2014.00146/full

Morse, Melvin. *Closer to the Light: Learning from the Near-Death Experiences of Children.* New York: Ivy Books, 1991.

————. *Where God Lives: The Science of the Paranormal and How Our Brains Are Linked to the Universe.* New York, NY: Cliff Street Books, 2000.

Nelson, Bradley. *The Emotion Code: How to Release Your Trapped Emotions for Abundant Health, Love, and Happiness.* Mesquite, NV: Wellness Unmasked, 2007.

Newton, Michael. *Journey of Souls: Case Studies of Life Between Lives.* St. Paul, MN: Llewellyn, 1994.

————. *Destiny of Souls: New Case Studies of Life Between Lives.* St. Paul, MN: Llewellyn, 2000.

————. *Life Between Lives: Hypnotherapy for Spiritual Regression.* St. Paul, MN: Llewellyn, 2004.

————. *Memories of the Afterlife: Life Between Lives Stories of Personal Transformation, With Case Studies by Members of the Newton Institute.* St. Paul, MN: Llewellyn, 2009.

Oliver, Sam. 2007. "Caring About Others." Ezine Articles. ezinearticles.com/?Caring- About-Others&id=822785

Osis, Karlis. "Deathbed Observations by Physicians and Nurses." *Parapsychological Monographs.* 3 (1961) Parapsychological Foundation.

Parnia, Sam and Peter Fenwick. "Near Death Experiences in Cardiac Arrest: Visions of a Dying Brain or Visions of a New Science of Consciousness." *Resuscitation.* 2002 Jan: 52(1): 5-11.

Parnia, Sam. *Erasing Death: The Science That is Rewriting the Boundaries Between Life and Death.* New York, NY: Harper Collins, 2013.

Palmieri, Arianna, et al. "'Reality' of near-death-experience memories: evidence from a psychodynamic and electrophysiological integrated study." PubMed.gov. US National Library of Medicine. National Institutes of Health. https://www.ncbi.nlm.nih.gov/pubmed/24994974

Paul, Apostle. *Living Bible.* Wheaton, IL: Tyndale House, 1973.

Penfield, Wilder. *Mystery of the Mind: A Critical Study of Consciousness and the Human Brain.* Princeton, NJ: Princeton University Press, 1978.

Piper, Don. *Ninety Minutes in Heaven: A True Story of Death and Life.* Grand Rapids, MI: Revell, 2004.

———. *Heaven is Real: Lessons on Earthly Joy–What Happened After Ninety Minutes in Heaven.* New York, NY: Penguin, 2007.

Renehan, Robert 1980. *Greek, Roman, and Byzantine Studies* 21:105-138

Ring, Kenneth and Sharon Cooper. *Mindsight: Near-Death and Out-of-Body Experiences in the Blind.* Palo Alto, CA: William James Center for Consciousness Studies, Institute of Transpersonal Psychology, 1999.

Ring, Kenneth. *Lessons from the Light: What We Can Learn from the Near-Death Experience.* Needham, MA: Moment Point Press, 2006.

Rosanoff, Nancy. *Intuition Workout: A Practical Guide to Discovering and Developing Your Inner Knowing.* Singapore, China: Asian Publishing, 1991.

Rosen, Eliot Jay. Eliot Jay Rosen's *Experiencing the Soul: Before Birth, During Life, After Death* . New Delhi, India: Motilal Banarsidass. 2005.

Satterfield, B. "Teachings Concerning the Veil of Forgetfulness." http://emp.byui.edu/SATTERFIELDB/Quotes/Veil%20of%20Forgetfulness.htm

"Seven Principles of Spirituality in the Workplace." 2009. http://www.itstime.com/rainbow.htm.

Schore, Allan. "Effects of a Secure Attachment, Relationship on Right Brain Development, Affect Regulation, and Infant Mental Health." Infant Mental Health Journal, Vol. 22(1-2), 7-66 (2001).

———. Chapter Twelve. "The Right Brain Implicit Self: A Central Mechanism of the Psychotherapy Change Process." *Knowing, Not-Knowing, and Sort-of-Knowing.* London, England: Karnac Books, 2010.

Sheldrake, Rupert. *The Sense of Being Stared At and Other Unexplained Powers of the Human Mind.* New York, NY: Three Rivers Press, 2004.

Siegel, Daniel. *Mindsight: The New Science of Personal Transformation.* New York, NY: Bantam Books, 2010.

Stanford Encyclopedia of Philosophy. 2016. History of Trinitarian Doctrines. https://plato.stanford.edu/entries/trinity/trinity-history.html

Stepanek, Mattie. Wikipedia. en.wikipedia.org/wiki/Mattie_Stepanek

Stevenson, Ian. *Unlearned Language: New Studies in Xenoglossy,* Charlottesville, VA: University of Virginia Press, 1984.

————. *Children Who Remember Previous Lives: A Question of Reincarnation.* Jefferson, NC: McFarland & Company, 2000.

————. "Dr. Ian Stevenson's Reincarnation Research." Division of Perceptible Studies, Health Sciences Center, University of Virginia, Charlottesville, VA 22908 https://www.near-death.com/reincarnation/research/ian-stevenson.html.

Storm, Howard. *My Descent Into Death: A Second Chance at Life.* New York, NY: Doubleday, 2005.

Sudden Cardiac Arrest Foundation (SCAF). http://www.sca-aware.org/about-the-sudden-cardiac-arrest-foundation

Terrafina. www.insnet.org/ins_press.rxml?id=3244&photo=.

Tymns, Michael. *The Afterlife Revealed.* Guildford, UK: White Crow Books, 2011.

van Lommel, Pim. *Consciousness Beyond Life: The Science of the Near-Death Experience.* San Francisco, CA: HarperOne, 2011.

Van Praagh, James. *Adventures of the Soul: Journeys Through the Physical and Spiritual Dimensions.* New York, NY: Hay House, 2014.

Wade, Jenny. *Changes of Mind.* Albany, NY: State of New York University Press, 1996.

Wade, Jenny. 1998. "Two Voices from the Womb: Evidence for Physically Transcendent and a Cellular Source of Fetal Consciousness." *Birth Psychology* 13: 123-148.

————. 1998. "Physically Transcendent Awareness: A Comparison of the Phenomenology of Consciousness Before Birth and After Death." *Journal of Near-Death Studies* 16:249-275.

Wambach, Helen. *Life Before Life.* New York, NY: Bantam Books, 1979.

Weiss, Brian. *Many Lives, Many Masters: The Story of a Prominent Psychiatrist, His Young Patient, and the Past-Life Therapy That Changed Both Their Lives.* New York, NY: Fireside Books, 1988.

————. *Through Time Into Healing.* New York, NY: Simon & Schuster, 1992.

————. *Only Love Is Real: A Story of Soulmates Reunited.* New York, NY: Warner, 1997.

————. *Messages From the Masters: Tapping Into the Power of Love.* New York, NY: Warner Books, 2000.

————. *Same Soul, Many Bodies: Discover the Healing Power of Future Lives Through Progression Therapy.* New York, NY: Free Press, 2004.

Whitton, Joel, and Joe Fisher. *Life Between Life.* Garden City, NY: Doubleday, 1986.

Wolf, Fred Alan. "The Quantum Physical Communication Between the Self and the Soul." *Noetic Journal* Volume 2, No. 2, April, 1999.